THE NOAH PARADOX

The Noah Paradox

Time as Burden, Time as Blessing

CAROL OCHS

University of Notre Dame Press
Notre Dame   London

Copyright © 1991 by
University of Notre Dame Press
Notre Dame, Indiana 46556
All Rights Reserved
Manufactured in the United States of America

Library of Congress Cataloging-in-Publication Data

Ochs, Carol.
    The Noah paradox : time as burden, time as blessing /
Carol Ochs.
        p.   cm.
    Includes bibliographical references.
    ISBN 0-268-01470-1
    1. Spiritual life. 2. Noah (Biblical figure) 3. Time—
Religious aspects. 4. Jewish way of life. I. Title.
    BL624.A3 1991
    291.4—dc20   90-50969
                                                          CIP

To the memory of

Julius Ochs

who survived the Flood with deepened faith

The Noah Paradox

Preface

Our eyes open slowly in the gray dawn and we begin to recollect all the suffering from which we gained temporary release during a night's sleep: physical deterioration, separation from those we love, doubt that our lives are meaningful, and awareness of suffering all around us. Perhaps the first commandment should read "Do not become weary!" Too many of the problems we wrestle with each day are the same ones we faced ten years ago. Not only (it seems) have we not learned anything new, we keep relearning the same things over and over.

It is with a new sympathy and appreciation, then, that we hear the "grumblings" of the Children of Israel in the wilderness. They had to survive the incalculable hardships of slavery, the terror of their flight from Egypt, and the perils of a journey across the Sea of Reeds (Red Sea), only to face a daily quest for food and water while making their way through a harsh desert. The repetitive story of their wandering in the wilderness instructs us: journeys have setbacks—do not become weary! The old problems recur. Solving them requires that *we* become new, and becoming new is the subject of this book.

I have always had a need to control. I was taught early on to plan in advance, outline my work, overprepare. It was an important lesson for someone who was to carry on full-time graduate work on a part-time schedule. Control and preparedness have been very important, but increasingly it is the lesson of releasing control that has changed my life.

What I have learned about trusting the incursions in my life—those "breakthrough" moments when I let go of my own plans to experience a deeper wisdom—has come less from verbal instruction and more from witnessing these phenomena in the way certain people have lived their lives.

My father, Herman Blumenthal, was the teacher who taught me to do my homework the moment I came home from school, to foresee all contingencies, and to adhere to a strict self-discipline. But it was Herman Blumenthal the artist who showed me that even after he had primed the canvas and outlined his subject in blue, the painting that followed might take on unexpected forms that surprised and delighted him. I too outline my subject, though with words on paper rather than blue paint on canvas. My original outline for this book has little to do with the pages that follow. During the writing, the book took on an unexpected shape, and I knew enough to let it surprise and delight me.

For my father-in-law, Julius Ochs, religious observance determined at what hours he would pray and what form his worship would take. But the openness to joy that he maintained showed me that while the forms might be controlled, the content was a gift freely experienced.

I have learned the most about these incursions in the domain of love. I spent my late childhood fantasizing about the person I would love. The crucial word is "fantasizing"—I was trying to bring control to an area that has little to do with control. I had my list of physical, intellectual, and emotional attributes. I have learned about the unexpected delight of love through sharing life with my husband, Michael Ochs, for over thirty years. Doing so has taught me that someone can lack many attributes I had listed as essential but still cause me to be filled with wonder. The otherness that infuriated was the same otherness that refreshed, nourished, and transformed me.

My colleague and friend David Burrell suggested that I write on the Jewish concept of grace. That, I thought, was a wonderful idea for a work to be written later, since the book I was writing was already well outlined. Only now that it is finished do I realize that I was writing about grace all along.

The creative process, or spiritual adventure, or way of love, is unlike other self-improvement programs in that it transforms the self. If I take up aerobics, vocabulary building, or dieting, I will become healthier, gain a larger vocabulary, or a thinner body. But when I enter into the transformative way, the very *I* that set out with the goal in mind is changed. Those of us who have lived as disciplined and controlled five-year planners find this idea frightening. But deeper than any fear is a growing trust. Trust entails not only an absence of skepticism but a transfer of allegiance, and even an identification with what surprises and delights us.

In addition to the grace-filled lives that I saw in my father and father-in-law, and that I enjoy daily with my husband, I have found other sources of support for my work. My students at Simmons College have been important teachers for me. I prepare and overprepare as usual for my classes, but then something on the periphery of my agenda may attract the students' attention and take us on an excursion that is genuinely novel and profitable for us all. I have benefited from frequent talks with Sebastian Moore. Margaret Rhodes and Floyd Barbour continue to show me the many aspects of friendship. I have gained much from the fellowship of the Society for Values in Higher Education, especially the discussion group "Struggling with Religious Tradition" and the late-night folksinging.

Introduction

I remember my father-in-law, with his young grandchildren around him, admonishing the glasses he had pushed onto his forehead, "Don't fall down!" and the helpless laughter of his grandchildren as he wiggled his forehead and the glasses slid down to the tip of his nose. "Again! Again!" they invariably shouted, and once again he would push his glasses onto his forehead and warn them, "Don't fall down!" My father-in-law was wildly in love with his grandchildren. In response to their prodding, he drew funny sketches and made his violin bow leap across the strings. I watched him not only with love, and with pride that I had borne two of his grandchildren, but with wonder. What had allowed him to re-engage in life and give himself so completely to these new loves?

My father-in-law had fled Nazi Germany in August 1939, leaving behind a way of life, a cultural heritage, and a self-understanding as an educated, upper-middle-class German citizen that was no longer appropriate for him in his new status as a Jewish refugee. He had left behind friends and people he had thought were friends, and years would pass before he could come to terms with his new life in the United States. But more than all of that, he left behind a world that no longer existed. Never again could he complacently believe that fine education and good taste in music would forestall destruction. Never again could he take for granted the friendship of neighbors and colleagues. Yet there he sat, surrounded by another generation, delighting in them and evoking their delight.

1

We live in a difficult time, for we are all too aware that the same technology that has helped save lives has also given us the capacity for self-destruction through nuclear disaster, toxic waste, depleted ozone layer. The air we breathe and the planet we live on are threatened by the life styles we have developed. The more we know about such threats, the more fearful we become. Our fears are expressed through drug and alcohol abuse, the suicide of our teenagers, and the frenetic activity of our young adults. What, then, can be our source of energy, affirmation, and commitment in a world in which our growing knowledge often leads to mounting fear and depression?

Fears concerning potential destruction exist at all levels in our world: planet, nation, work community, neighborhood, family, and self. On the broadest level, we fear that we won't be able to control the technology we have created, that sometime before we die of natural causes we will be wiped out in an accidental or deliberate nuclear holocaust. On the level of country or community, we may view the growing cancers of homelessness, drug abuse, poverty, and crime with a sense of overwhelming weariness. Sometimes our focus is narrowed and our world limited to our family or our colleagues at work. The relationships in these worlds are complex, and the same problems constantly reappear. The problems recur, but our energy diminishes. Sometimes our world is reduced to ourselves, as when we stand before our doctors and hear them declare that a foreign and dangerous growth has to be removed.

We think we are living in a time wholly unprecedented in human history. Never before have we had the capacity to destroy the entire world. We do not know how to respond to such a threat. But we are not the first to contemplate the possible destruction of the world. In the next major story in Genesis after that of Cain and Abel, Noah experiences the Great Flood, which destroys his entire civilization. We can use this story to help deal with the fears of destruction in our lives. We can also use our own experiences and fears to help illuminate the story. In reading the text, we realize that while Noah may sharply criticize the society in which he lives, nevertheless, he does not want it destroyed—only changed. However much he may have despised the world in which he grew up, it is the world he knows and the only one he can envision. As a result of the Flood, he loses a way of life, a cultural heritage, and a self-understanding as a member of his society. He loses friends and people he had thought were friends. But, above all, he leaves behind a world that no longer exists. Never again can he complacently believe that the good things of the earth are his to enjoy without fear of loss or destruction. When the flood waters abate, Noah steps out of the ark into a world devoid of all the landmarks that had signified "home" to him in the past. He is charged by God with re-creating and rebuilding society, even though all he has to aid him is his memory of a world that was fatally flawed, together with some vague stirrings of his imagination: visions of a better world. Then God makes a covenant with Noah:

> Never again will I doom the earth because of man, since the devisings of man's mind are evil from his youth; nor will I ever destroy every living being, as I have done.

> So long as the earth endures,
> Seedtime and harvest,
> Cold and heat,
> Summer and winter,
> Day and Night
> Shall not cease.[1]

Noah plants the first vineyard. He subsequently drinks wine from the vineyard and becomes drunk. The two events, God's covenant with Noah and Noah's drinking, are intimately connected: Noah drinks in order to obliterate his awareness of the covenant. While the promise that time will continue on forever may seem reassuring, for those who have survived the destruction of great masses of people or have endured some other monstrous horror, once is enough. The thought that they may have to face not one but a series of trials can be overwhelming. By God's promise humans would be spared future floods, not because the situation has been corrected but because it is incorrigible: "Never again will I doom the earth because of man, since the devisings of man's mind are evil from his youth."

Like Noah, we know that we are flawed. We must live flawed lives and live with the awareness of our own flaws and those of our world. In order to relieve his grief, Noah "doctored" himself by drinking wine. He had the correct diagnosis of his depression—an awareness of the burden of time—but he chose the wrong cure, though the reasoning behind his choice is interesting. He recognized that, in order to endure his awareness of the ongoingness of time, he needed to change his perception, so he chose inebriation, a form of altered perception.

As survivors of the Holocausts of World War II, we stand where Noah stood, knowing that we are flawed and that our lives are a series of trials and ongoing struggles. We feel Noah's pain, but we should reject Noah's solution (which had disastrous consequences for Noah; according to biblical commentaries, it resulted in his castration by his son). What is to be our response to this situation?

In this book we will examine what I call the Noah Paradox: the mixed blessing entailed by the ongoingness of time. Having endured devastations and floods, we now seek a way to experience God's covenant as an unmixed blessing. We are asked to rejoice, but in our present state of mind we cannot. Somehow we must learn how to overcome our fears and anger. If there is to be a solution to the Noah Paradox, it cannot take the form of "more of the same." We require not a quantitative change—more time—but a qualitative change—a transformation of the self, what Aristotle calls "becoming other." Becoming other is, by definition, not more of the same. Something genuinely new must be introduced; either we must change, or we must change our relationship to the world.

The search for a solution to the Noah Paradox is an individual one. We must each find our own way to courage and recommitment. In the face of someone else's suffering we should be silent. In that respect, Job's comforters did well for one week: "They sat with him on the ground for seven days and seven nights and no one said a word to him, for they saw that his anguish was very great" (Job 2:13). But the comforters couldn't remain silent. They felt a need to answer Job or perhaps to quiet their own doubts, and at that point their "comfort" became another of Job's trials. So the paths to spiritual transformation discussed in this book are intended for those who choose to try them out in their own lives. They provide neither general justifications for suffering nor answers to the problem of evil. They are accounts of what *we* can do to deal with Noah's Paradox.

In searching for renewal, affirmation, and courage we will examine three paths to change: creativity, spirituality, and love. We will begin by looking at God's creativity. By carefully examining the creative process described in Genesis 1, we can discern terror, self-giving, and love, all of which we will recognize as components of our own creativity. In thus identifying our creativity with God's, we will recognize our contact with God. Understanding God's creativity can give us courage to go on, because we can reaffirm that we are created in the image of God. Then we can see our own creative possibilities by reading Genesis 1 as a road map for our lives.

My father was an artist. I remember waking in the morning and testing the air for the smells of linseed oil and turpentine. If they were there, I tiptoed quickly down the hall to his room to see what magic had occurred on the canvas during the night. Sometimes there would be a new canvas with ideas outlined in blue paint. No matter how often I viewed these outlines I could never envision the finished painting. That was because my father did not restrict himself to his original outlines when he painted. He was open to a progressive revelation of what the painting needed.

Once, after examining a drawing I had made on paper, he suggested that I do a painting based on the drawing. He set up a canvas and lent me his oils. I stared and stared at the canvas but was unable to bring the brush to it. I spent a long time squeezing out gobs of different colors on the palette, postponing the moment when I would have to apply the paint to the canvas. When I finally overcame my paralysis I couldn't stop and painted colors on top of other colors, my original drawing lost beneath the frenzy of paint. The result of this experience discouraged any further pursuit of painting, but it did not affect my fascination with the creative process. Even now, thinking of painting brings on the excitement that vivified my father and reminds me of the terror I felt in staring at the empty canvas. I think of the disciplined yet free stroke of his brush and of my own unchecked splattering of paint. And I think of the artistic road map that he intuitively followed and that I lacked.

We stand at a crossroad: we have witnessed destruction and we want to stop, cover our heads, and retreat. But our imperative is to move ahead and create, and the creation account in Genesis shows us how we can do so and what we can hope for. Creativity is both our calling and the process that transforms us.

However, our true task is not to create but to re-create. We are aware of the flaws in our current civilization—modernity, contemporary morality, runaway technology, naïveté about our political system, and excessive optimism about most people's capacity for compassion. If we are to re-create the world in a better way, at least within ourselves, how can we go about it?

The Hebrew Scriptures recount other major catastrophes, besides the Great Flood, that allow us to examine the re-creation process. With the siege of Jerusalem, the Babylonian exile, and the destruction of the Temple, the Jewish people lost all the symbols whose meaning and value had sustained them. In that context, Ezekiel has two visions. The first concludes with "the appearance of the bow [that] shines in the clouds on a day of rain, such is the appearance of the surrounding radiance" (Ezek. 1:28), the sign of God's covenant with Noah. Later we will see how Ezekiel, faced with the Noah Paradox, experiences another vision that shows us how to persist and rebuild after destruction. In this instance, his second vision is of the New Jerusalem and includes a detailed description of a new Temple. The vision is not a look backward at the Temple that was destroyed, nor is it a blueprint for the new Temple to be built. The Temple in the vision is a symbol of creation, a model of the soul, and the locus for our meeting with the Holy Presence. The vision reminds us of the Presence that gives us the courage to go on, telling us destruction does not destroy the possibility of experiencing God's Presence.

The second path to change is the spiritual way. The vulnerability and weariness produced by the Noah Paradox may tempt us to seek a spiritual alternative, either fleeing this world or taking refuge in some false but comforting doctrine. But the true spiritual way is not risk-free, notwithstanding the simplified version often portrayed in popular literature. It is as demanding as the creative way and, like the latter, changes us. The five stages of the spiritual way are outlined in the biblical story of the Exodus from Egypt: The Israelites *awaken* to their enslaved condition in Egypt, are *purged* by their wandering in the wilderness, experience *illumination* at Mount Sinai, undergo the *dark night of the soul* in the incident of the Golden Calf, and achieve *union* in their building of the Tabernacle.

The third path to change is the way of love. Love is as demanding as creativity and spirituality. It takes us outside ourselves and renews our sense of purpose. The biblical text that charts this way is the Song of Songs, though a full picture of love can be gained only by reading this book in conjunction with the Book of Lamentations, because love entails openness not only to growth and joy but to loss and suffering. Love is a powerful aid in resolving the Noah Paradox; it also represents an alternative way of thinking about the Exodus. So we will study the Song of Songs with two purposes in mind: first, to explore the way of love as a means of defusing the Noah Paradox; second, to gain a fresh understanding of the Exodus.

Having delineated the three ways of change—creativity, spirituality, and love—we have shown only the bright part of the picture. We must also deal with the reality of catastrophes and the destructive element that is present along each of these three paths. After my first experience with painting I might have removed some of the paint from the canvas (an act I now recognize as being just as creative as applying the paint) or I might have reprimed the canvas and begun again. Instead, I chose not to paint. But in giving up painting, I did not give up creating, and I have had to deal with the pain of re-creating in other endeavors.

One form of creation is forming a relationship. Forming my earliest relationships was not unlike facing my blank canvas: for a long time paralysis and terror; then a frenzied attempt to open up to the other; then, after time, a realization that if a relationship is to nourish me and give me a joint project to contribute to over a long period of time, it will have to be re-formed. Using the metaphor of painting, the canvas will have to be cleaned with turpentine and repainted. The "turpentine" in this case is honesty, which can bring us more deeply in touch with our growing self as it is revealed in relationship. It can also destroy a friendship that is based only on politeness and amiability. Creativity is risky, and the attempt at meaningful re-creation may be destructive. I have been fortunate in some of my re-created relationships. After the initial pain and discomfort, something more beautiful has emerged, and through such experiences I have perceived the relationship between creativity and destruction.

Having explored the role of destruction in creativity, spirituality, and love, we can reconceive the formative stories of the biblical tradition. The God of Exodus is the God of the Flood, and the story of the Exodus can now be understood as the story of the Flood. Both these stories, in turn, are different formulations of the Song of Songs. At different points in our lives we may describe the essential story as one of creativity, spirituality, or love. Just as we can understand the different stories as variations on one basic story, we can see that the three transformative ways are essentially the same path.

This study of the three ways of change is not presented as a source of comfort. It does not lead to an easy assurance that all will be well or that what we have suffered is somehow meaningful. Rather than seeking comfort, we must seek a way to renew our spiritual commitment and courage, which have been eroded by constant flooding. Energy and courage do not guarantee that our lives will be happy and protected, nor do they let us dismiss our very real suffering as being a means

1. *In the Beginning: God's Creativity*

The Noah Paradox challenges our creativity. Let us start by examining God's creativity and use what we learn as a road map for our own creative process.

The beginning is pregnant with the end. Within the very elements of creation lie the factors that give rise to the Noah Paradox. And perhaps within these same elements lie the factors that give rise to the solution. We raise the same questions of God that we did of our parents: Did you want me? Was I an accident or deeply longed for? Were you satisfied with what you got? And we push back for an answer to the unasked question: Were we made of good stuff? Is there an inherent flaw in our formulation or do we really have the possibility of being good?

If the account of Creation is to answer the Noah Paradox, that is, if it is to allow us to experience the ongoingness of time as a blessing, then we must discover the transformative force of creativity—its capacity to make all things new. Let us examine the account of Creation as it is given in Genesis 1.

Day One: Chaos as a Necessary Stage

When God began to create the heaven and the earth—the earth being unformed and void, with darkness over the surface of the deep. . . .

We tend to interpret these first lines of Genesis as describing a condition that God must *overcome* before undertaking creation. Instead, we should recognize that chaos, darkness, and void constitute an important and necessary first stage in the creative process. Chaos, or formlessness, is needed because if something already has a form it cannot be created, only re-created. It is formlessness that invites the many possibilities of creation. The darkness over the surface of the deep has the potential for new life. The void, too, is essential because creation occurs in an unoccupied space, a space free to receive the new creation. Our own thoughts turn away from this image of chaos, darkness, and void. We fear entering mentally into this process, but creation entails effort and sacrifice.

The breath of God hovering over the face of the waters—

Here we get a sense of intimacy. God is close, nearby, concerned, hovering. As we will be seeing, the path of creativity coincides with the path of love. And in looking at the creative process we discern a notion of intimacy.

Let there be light.

Light, which is both the first creation of God and the prime precondition for the rest of creation, can be understood as the consciousness behind the rest of creation, analogous to the "inner light" of our own consciousness. The light referred to in this first day of Creation is not physical light. Physical light comes into being with the creation of the sun, moon, and stars on the fourth day of Creation. The fact that consciousness was created first affirms the belief that creation is neither accidental nor the result of chance meetings of particles. Nor is it the unconscious overflowing of the Creator (as emanationists believe). Creation is a thoughtful, deliberate process.

God saw that the light was good, and God separated the light from the darkness. God called the light Day, and the darkness God called Night.

As part of the creative process of the first day, God saw, evaluated, separated, and named. All these processes are forms of creativity. The first process, seeing, entails the capacity to imagine new possibilities, a major step in creativity. The model of perception described here is not one that forces recalcitrant matter into some preexistent mold; instead it is one of openness, waiting for the intrinsic nature of a substance or situation to reveal itself. Perception all too frequently consists not only in taking in sense data but in ordering that data in terms of past experiences and future expectations. When our hopes and fears distort our openness often we cannot perceive the true nature of creation.

The second creative process of the first day is evaluating: seeing the light as *good*. Evaluation is needed to give the creation meaning. The creator cannot fail to evaluate; not to evaluate is not to care, and one must care enough to have standards. The evaluative process affirms that value is inherent in creation. God does not simply, by fiat, declare the light to be good, God *judges* that it is good.

The third creative process of the first day is separating; separating night from day (recognizing their differences) and separating creation from the Creator. This last act reminds us that an important aspect of creativity is letting go of the creation. If we are truly separate from our Creator, we can choose the extent of our distance, the direction in which we will go, the way we will follow. Separation is an essential component of creation, but one that bears great cost to the creator. We can try to understand this part of creation by examining our own reaction to separation. Separation usually frightens us, so we tend to resist it. But in retrospect we often discover that some of our most significant growth has occurred because of separation. In order to nurture a child, we must be connected to the child. The connection is useful and necessary as long as it fosters growth and life. But when the child is ready to take on responsibility for its own life and grow into adulthood, it is time for parent and child to separate.

The fourth creative process taken on the first day is naming. Naming draws distinctions and fosters creations. God's act of naming has creative force. Naming correctly joins the head and the heart, because to love someone is to know or bestow their real name. We will be called by many names during our lives, but the One who truly knows us knows our real name.

We turned to the Creation account in Genesis in order to renew our courage and transform our doubts in the face of the Noah Paradox, so our task must be to discern how these four creative processes—seeing, evaluating, separating, and naming—are related to transformation and renewal. To begin with, creation entails a true perception of another. To "see" an illusion is not to derive nourishment and renewal but to be limited by our own fantasies. Second, creation requires measuring the creation against a standard. Doing so does not negate God's infinite patience and forgiveness, or our own when we are the creator, but there must be a standard. Third, creation means respect and reverence for separation, even though we fear it. Finally, creation requires a deep knowing (naming) of the creature's true essence.

Day Two: Separation and the Creation of Space

God said, "Let there be an expanse in the midst of the water, that it may separate water from water." God made the expanse, and it separated the water which was below the expanse from the water which was above the expanse. And it was so. God called the expanse *sky.*

The creative process of separation is continued here. In addition, the concept of space is introduced, specifically, that of *particular* space or location. Creation can be understood, in part, as the process of recognizing the rightful place of things. But place itself is a concept that can exist on several levels. In the most obvious sense, place is a spatial or geographical concept, although even the geographical notion of place is not a simple one. For instance, people become attached to specific geographical locations and consider them sacred or "home." Place can also be an economic and vocational concept, as in the expressions "one's position in life" and "one's place in the economic or political or social order." In addition to introducing the concept of location, the creation of space allows for such concepts as fullness and emptiness. These terms, which refer to simple empirical states, can also be used to describe value standards. Thus, Day Two of Creation contains perspectives that could potentially deaden or renew. Space has been created, but it is left to us to name it holy or not and to rejoice in its fullness or to bemoan its emptiness.

Day Three: The Creative Force of Limit

God said, "Let the water below the sky be gathered into one area, that the dry land may appear."

Reading this passage, we can see that limitation is a significant part of creation. The dry land appears, not as the result of a new creation, but as a result of the restriction or limiting of matter. Creativity is not simply fecundity. It occurs within limits, such as those imposed by the span of one's life, the frame of a painting, or the preexisting conventions of a musical form. One of the most powerful uses of creativity is the restriction of the process. For instance, we don't compose note after note forever in order to write a piece of music. We allow for rests between phrases to give form and sense to the composition. Neither do we fill every inch of a canvas with paint; instead, we let the unpainted spaces heighten the impact of the colors. We don't speak without pause; the silence around our words can give them a deeper significance. We create, pause, then create again. This limiting of self-expression to allow for the freedom of the creation is a major part of creativity. We usually think of creativity in terms of a series of positive processes, but limitation is a positive aspect as well. We need to recognize when to teach and when to assume that the lesson has been taught. Pauses between teaching are needed so that students will have time to assimilate the lesson and make it their own. God must limit each creation so that the creations don't overwhelm one another; more significantly, God must limit the Divine creative force so that it doesn't overwhelm each separate creation.

Day Four: The Creation of Time

> God said, "Let there be lights in the expanse of the sky to separate day from night; they shall serve as signs for the set times—the days and the years."

The text describing the fourth day illustrates a way to mark time and invest it with meaning. The ability to mark time allows us to set periods of time apart as special or sacred, to note special occasions, and even to create memory. It lets us use time for creative division of our lives. The marking of time is related to the awareness of limitation and can therefore be either enlivening or deadening. We often deal with limitations in our lives, yet in order for us to recognize limitation we must be able to contrast it with lack of limitation: the infinite. If everything in our lives were limited, we would have no concept of limit. All we know must pass away, yet something endures and preserves that which is known so that it does not become lost. In reflecting on our limitations, and our finiteness, and our ability to recognize limitation, we can find God.

Day Five: Blessing and Releasing

God created the great sea monsters, and all the living creatures of every kind that creep, which the waters brought forth in swarms; and all the winged birds of every kind. And God saw that this was good. God blessed them, saying, "Be fertile and increase, fill the waters in the seas, and let the birds increase on the earth."

It is on this fifth day that the word *blessed* is used for the first time. In this context we recognize that blessing is bestowing on a creature the possibility of carrying on creation (being fertile, increasing, and filling the waters). The freedom inherent in the first two days of Creation is taken to its ultimate in bestowing on creatures the capacity to carry on the creation. We recognize the stunning identity of blessing and creativity, and we are tempted to consider all the uses of the word *blessing* to see if the identity holds. And then we turn away from texts to our own experience. Have our own moments of blessedness been moments of creativity?

Day Six: In the Creator's Image

And God created humankind in God's image, in the image of God did God create it, male and female did God create them.

In order to understand more fully what it means for us to be made in the image of God, we must review the events of the first five days of Creation, because our image of God is that of the God of Creation. Liberation and redemption are concepts that came long after the world was created, even though they may be recognizable in the early stages of creation. However, our explicit image of God lies within the first five days of Creation:

1. emptiness, openness, waiting;
2. calling forth, seeing, evaluating;
3. separating, naming;
4. limiting, placing; marking of time; and
5. blessing and releasing the creatures' own creativity.

Day Seven: The Creation of Rest

The last day of Creation is not the sixth day, but the seventh:

> The heaven and the earth were finished, and all their array. On the seventh day God finished the work which God had been doing, and God ceased on the seventh day from all the work which God had done. And God blessed the seventh day and declared it holy, because on it God ceased from all the work of creation which God had done.

Rest plays a vital role in creation. It links the themes of restricting the act of creation, of creating space for reflection, and of marking time as sacred. Samuel Terrien suggests an additional significance of the seventh day:

> The ceremonial evocation of the "genesis" of the universe (Gen. 1:1–2:4a) was told, not as a cosmogony destined to satisfy para-scientific curiosity, but as a proclamation of the holiness of the Sabbath within the creative act of God. The story of the genesis of the universe does not belong

to didactic or epic literature. It constitutes the opening of a living *Torah*. Because it climactically leads to the divine pronouncement of the sacrality of time, it ushers in a new mode of presence. The creator may seem to be absent from history, but he is present in the cosmos and offers man a means of participating in divine creativity.[1]

In other words, the creation of rest allows the creatures made in God's image to experience God's presence. If we cannot experience God's presence in a sacred place, because the Temple has been destroyed or because we no longer stand at Mount Sinai, we can experience God's presence in time, in the weekly experience of reenacting the seventh day of creation. We, too, are world makers, and in our creation of worlds we often become discouraged, overwhelmed, and confused. But when we pause in our act of creation and step back to reflect, we find that our smaller worlds of meaning are lifted into the framework of the larger creation. We sense that we are not alone and that we create because we have been created. And in that quiet pause we sense the presence of our Creator.

In examining the biblical description of Creation we see that the division of the process into seven days or stages is arbitrary. For example, on Day One we encounter the concept of separation, even though separation as a major mode of creativity is not introduced until Day Two. On Day Two, space, with its implied notion of boundaries, is introduced, but it is only on Day Three that the notion of boundaries and limits becomes a major theme. Although the concept of limitation is introduced on Day Three, time, an essential limit for mortals, is created only on Day Four. While the division of Creation into seven stages may be arbitrary, certain aspects of the process are clearly established. Emptiness, waiting, blessing, and releasing are all essential aspects of the creative way.

Ten Creations of the First Day

We can also study the creative way delineated in
Genesis by examining the five pairs of creations of the
first day. According to the Midrash, these were: *tohu*
and *bohu* (translated as "chaos" and "void"); light and
darkness; heaven and earth; wind and water; and measure of day and measure of night.[2]

Tohu and Bohu

Tohu and *bohu* are translated as chaos and void. We
recognize them in the daily cycle of sleep. As we fall
asleep, we enter the dark world of *tohu* and *bohu*. When
we awaken, we emerge from chaos and void. Hence each
day is a re-creation that must be preceded by chaos and
emptiness.

The Midrash asks, "What is *tohu?* Something that
perturbs people and becomes *bohu*. What is *bohu?* Something that contains reality."[3] This typically cryptic passage informs us that a process is taking place, one that
involves change and ends in reality. *Tohu* and *bohu*
demonstrate two aspects of chaos: the *sense* of chaos
before we have ordered and formed our creations; and
the *need* for chaos so as to avoid premature structuring
of that which needs to flow freely for a while. Logically
understanding the need for chaos can help us deal with
the unease we feel in recognizing that the first require-
ments for creation are chaos, emptiness, and letting go
of previous boundaries and structures.

Light and Darkness

According to the Zohar on Genesis, there are forty-
five sorts of light distributed in the world.[4] But God is
credited with creating darkness as well. The creation of
darkness begins the process of stripping away the fea-
tures distinguishable in the light. Light gives shape,

definition, and order, all of which must be removed
before a new creation can emerge. Light is associated
with life because it has warmth and other properties
needed for producing and supporting growth. But darkness is no less essential for life. For instance, it is in the
dark warmth of the soil that seeds germinate. We recognize the life-giving properties of darkness even as we
acknowledge that darkness is associated with death.
There are two lessons here: the necessary role of darkness, and the fact that darkness is not the negation of
light.

We must willingly give up control—a kind of death—
in order to genuinely create, because creation does not
come out of our *willfulness*, or holding onto control, but
out of our *willingness*, or giving up control. We should
accept a healthy balance between light and darkness,
and resist our tendency to always seek light instead of
recognizing the benefits of darkness. Western civilization
since the Enlightenment has tried to extend light and
exert power over all it does not understand. In the
process, we have lost the humility and wonder we should
feel in confronting the unknown.

The creation of light *and* darkness serves to remind
us that we are not simply creatures of reason. Our
reason is fallible and may not even be our best attribute.
The things we know through reason are not those we
especially treasure. For instance, value, love, commitment, and meaning do not lie in the rational domain,
and that is why they are the subjects of such fierce
controversies. People do not go to war over the length
of the sides of a triangle, but they do over love of
country, commitment to language, culture, or tradition,
or interpretation of religious doctrine. Clearly, reason is
important but not all-sufficient. Beyond reason lie hope
and charity. Hope is saying "yes" to life, insisting that
all is meaningful and serves a good purpose, finding
something of value in everything. Charity is hope ad-

dressed to others—individuals and groups of people—
and assuming that there is something good at work in
all institutions and communities.

True, reason can foster charity, but not because we
love for a reason. Our rational involvement with a
question can lead us to wonder at the intricacies of the
elements involved. Through our concern and attention
we may even come to love that which we study, but our
love is not caused by reason but by our emotional
engagement.

In order to create we must enter the dark. Like the
light, darkness is at once both beneficent and dangerous.
We enter it best not with our intellect but with love
and with faith and hope, the fruits of love. Faith gives
us patience, keeps us receptive, warms and comforts us.
Hope leads us to believe that life has some greater
purpose, which we intend to foster. Love allows us to
interpret darkness in a positive manner.

Darkness remains the darkness. Faith, hope, and
charity do not dispel darkness and are not themselves
immune from the negative forces of darkness, which
attack love through fear, faith through skepticism, and
hope through despondency. But the positive forces of
darkness allow love to germinate, faith to grow, and
hope to warm. Contemplating the descriptions of light
and darkness in the Midrash can help us rediscover the
right balance between them and reexperience the gift
of darkness.

The second lesson suggested by God's dual creation
of light and darkness is that the apparent disparity
between them, as well as between life and death, is just
that—apparent but not real. We tend to associate light
with life and death with darkness, but the previous
discussion has shown that darkness is as essential for
life as light. A deeper lesson is hinted at here: things
that appear utterly opposite and opposed can be ultimately reconciled.

Heaven and Earth

We see the earth and we imagine heaven, and it is this dual vision that gives shape to our creativity. Life in heaven, as we might imagine it, would not be creative. But so too life on earth without a vision would be living without a dream, without a source for creativity. But the dual vision of earth and heaven gives us the setting and the inspiration for the work we are called upon to do.

The Jewish notion of heaven differs from both the Greek realm of the ideal forms and the Christian location for the afterlife. In the Jewish tradition, heaven is not even unlimited; its upper limit is water. Judaism makes reference to our dual vision in noting that people walk upright, rather than crawling, because they look up to heaven. In one of Kafka's parables, a man's arm is raised up to heaven and his feet are on the earth, depicting the tension of being human. The tension is sometimes resolved over time, as age makes us let go of the earth and move spiritually closer to heaven. But tension is akin to stretching and, in this context, may be considered a lifelong process. We are the union of above and below, heaven and earth. In Judaism, as well as in Plato's philosophy, we mediate between the worlds of *being* and *becoming*. We need to recognize the part of us that is unchanging and enduring, even as we accept the transitory nature of the rest. One Midrash attributes Adam's fall to his choosing to unify the lights of the lower world rather than his persisting in the more difficult task of unifying the lights of the upper world *with* those of the lower. As we recall from the light created on the first day, light refers to consciousness, not to physical energy. To think about life with only the consciousness of the timeless and enduring heavenly perspective is inadequate. To think about life from the perspective only of the changing day to day is similarly flawed. So Adam would have fallen had he chosen to unify the lights of the upper world alone; his task was to unite the two. As described in the biblical text, Adam failed to maintain the tension between upper and lower. His sin was distraction. The third pair of creations, heaven and earth, seems to hint at the lesson taught by the second pair, light and darkness: there can be no absolute distinction between the two elements in a pair.

Wind and Water

The creations wind and water must be fully understood in order to grasp the lessons they can teach us. *Ruach*, Hebrew for "wind," also means "breath" (as in "God breathed the breath of life into Adam") and "spirit." Every moment we are breathing we are experiencing our interconnection with the rest of life. We breathe air previously breathed by those around us. We breathe out to the grasses and trees. That which is inside us is outside us, around us, through us, and is both wind and spirit. Water is also vivifying, cleansing, and purifying. It, too, is both outside and inside us. It is essential for our being and well-being. Wind and water are the enspiriting, energizing, and life-giving forces of creation that are both internal and external to us.

Measure of Day and Measure of Night

Limitation transforms chaos to cosmos, so limitation in all its many forms is a creative force. Time is one kind of limitation. It is our limited life expectancy that makes us mortal. Meaning in a human life occurs because of an awareness of our mortality. We *transcend* our limitations by creating something immortal. We may create ideas that endure, works of art that participate in the timeless, values that are eternal. Psalm 90:12

hints at the same thing: "Teach us to count our days rightly, that we may obtain a wise heart." A wise heart is one that can love the timeless in the limited.

There is wisdom and creativity in knowing our limitations. For instance, we can see creativity in Abraham's awareness of the limits of life, in his mourning for Sarah. Abraham begins by lamenting and weeping for his deceased wife. These activities are the beginning of mourning, which is a complex creative process. Too often, mourning is stopped at the "pain-management" stage and not carried to the point at which the mourner can reclaim in new and transformed ways that which has been lost. Our incapacity to mourn fully results from our misuse of power. We try to control even the transformations that mourning offers by not willingly entering into the whole process, which eventually becomes a healing and creative one. Abraham's mourning proceeds beyond lamenting and weeping to the formal purchase of a burial site, Machpeleh, not only for Sarah but for himself. By this action, Abraham demonstrates that he has come face to face with his own mortality. Only then does he recognize that he must pass on his gifts, and he urgently charges his servant to seek a wife for Isaac.

Otherness

Our list of the ten creations of the first day does not include otherness, though the binary formulation of the list implies it. Otherness is essential for creativity. Our first experiences in life are encounters with otherness. We are physically separated from our mothers. We find out that there are events, beings, and consciousnesses that are independent of us. They do not mirror us, and we cannot control them. These beings, consciousnesses, and events impinge on our lives. Not only does the otherness of people sometimes impinge on us, but we have a sense that things could have been otherwise. We are responsible only in part for the way things are, and we can never calculate the full implications of any choice we make.

Otherness in Genesis is central to the discussion of separation and division, to the naming of creatures (*this* one as distinct from *that* one), to the repeated call to wander, and to the exhortation to remember the stranger who is other than you. We can take the call to Abraham as a call to make a covenant with otherness and to love it. The otherness of God is experienced first in the otherness of people. The call to love otherness is also a call to allow the other to be itself, that is, not to manipulate or deny the other's subjectivity. The other is not to be destroyed or cut off for all time. For example, Cain is spared, Ishmael persists, Esau is not destroyed, and the Egyptians are not completely wiped out. Neither should otherness be transformed into sameness. It must persist as otherness and be taken up into some larger whole.

We have difficulties in dealing with otherness, most especially the otherness of evil. The biblical view is expressed as: "I form light and create dark, I make peace and create evil" (Is. 45:7). We are willing to recognize darkness as part of the creative process, but we find it more difficult to accept the role of evil. The Bible teaches not the final destruction of evil but its integration in a balanced whole. That evil is not to be ultimately de-stroyed but joined with good provides us with the best example of God's creativity and the deliberate self-lim-itation of power. God could destroy evil; instead, God chooses to balance it with evil's "other," good. Power is exercised most frequently in the face of otherness. In our effort to defeat the other, we frequently take on the other's characteristics and become the very enemy we fear. But when otherness is understood to have a role in a larger system we do not deform ourselves in at-tempting to control it. Our tolerance of otherness involves the fear and chaos that are part of true creativity. Tolerance of evil may be a frightening experience, but we must not let fear defeat us. In rejecting fear, we choose life.

We have studied the Creation account in Genesis and observed the complexities of the creative process. We have recognized God's painful self-limitation of power for the sake of the independence and otherness of creation. We have noted the multiplicity of creative choices offered to us, in terms of space and place, light and darkness, fullness and emptiness, and ways to mark and give value to time. We saw the choices proliferate when we explored the tension between heaven and earth. And through it all, we see the characteristics of a creative way: the darkness, the implicit trust that allows us a multiplicity of choices, and the letting go which all lie at the heart of true humility.

2. In the Image of God: Our Creativity

As an approach to the Noah Paradox, we have explored the different types of creative processes that are part of the Creation. The exploration led to a discussion of the elements that make up the creative way. We discovered that when we are blessed, we are released to create, and that this mandate is reiterated in our being created in the image of God. Therefore, by creating we can encounter God.

It is difficult to fully examine our own creativity and to determine whether what we create has any value. It is simpler to bypass our creativity and focus on the products, such as paintings, sculptures, or poems. We tend to forget the creativity involved in nurturing relationships, granting forgiveness, and feeling joy.

The Creation and Nothing

We know that God created the meaning and value in our world. We can create similar worlds, but it is hard to know whether our worlds are connected to God's world. If they are not, then our worlds of meaning are illusory or even delusory. We fear that if we really explored our creativity we would find that we create nothing of lasting value. This fear deserves careful examination. The key to dealing with the fear rests in the word *nothing*. Traditionally, nothingness was thought to be terrifying. However, according to some mystical traditions one of God's names is Nothing, that is, *no thing*.[1]

God cannot be reduced to any definite limited thing, hence, God is no thing. But does this proof really counter our terror or is it merely a verbal trick? The statement that God is the great nothing may be justified conceptually, but it may also be confirmed experientially. In the process of contemplation, Dom Chapman reports, "You leave [your imagination] as nearly uncontrolled as possible, in order to have the will fixed on nothing in particular—which is God, of course."[2] He also states that "only in prayer can you get near [the image of death]— if the world ever falls away, and leaves you in infinity— which you can only describe as nothingness, though it is everything."[3] A contemporary Buddhist teacher expresses the same idea:

> Buddhism states specifically what we know for certain. It will not state that which is taken on faith. We can find this for ourselves—that [the eternal] is unborn and so forth—but we cannot state what it is. Therefore we call it Mu or "nothing" or "emptiness" or, as my master called it, "the immaculacy of emptiness," which is the fullest description I've ever bumped into.[4]

Nothingness is not only an idea, it is an experience— and a potentially terrifying one. Little by little we become less fearful of the experience, after we have witnessed repeated instances of its fruitfulness. Despite this reassurance, the experience of nothingness remains a frightening one. The fear is countered by a strong positive tradition that identifies nothing and nothingness with God. As our experience with nothingness grows, along with our trust in it, we find within or beyond it the very source of our creation and creativity.

Our negative view of nothingness and our fear that our creations are illusory must be addressed continually. One approach to the situation is to believe that the worlds of meaning we create *are* illusory and that recognizing this illusion is a form of liberation. In contrast,

Jewish tradition teaches that our world is both real and meaningful and that our individual struggles to uphold values, resist temptation, and contribute to the world are serious and important.

Two definitions of "nothing" need to be distinguished: (1) the experience of ultimate reality, which, since it is beyond anything we can conceive or imagine, is called "nothing" or the "desert of the Godhead"; and (2) the lack of any inherent meaning in the world, from which it follows that, in creating our ideas, values, and artifacts, we ourselves impose the only meaning the world can be said to have. The rabbis, aware of the fear that accompanies this second sense of "nothing," addressed it in a debate on whether heaven preceded earth or vice versa: "Heaven was created first and afterwards earth. . . . Earth was created first and afterwards Heaven. . . . Both were created at the same time."[5] If the earth were created at the same time as heaven, the earth would have meaning.

According to the account in Genesis, heaven and earth were both created, and both have the same source. What, then, is the difference between heaven and earth? In one view, the difference is spatial; heaven is above the earth. But since the terms "above" and "below" have meaning only with respect to the earth, spatial location has nothing to do with basic differences between heaven and earth. Another view holds that the difference involves time: heaven endures, while earth is ephemeral. But, according to Genesis, both are created, so neither is eternal. We also might think that the difference is one of value: heaven is the domain of true value, while earth is not. But there is nothing in Genesis to support that view. As the creation of the earth progresses, God repeatedly finds the earthly creations good.

What is really at stake in the talmudic debate about which came first, heaven or earth? "First" has three meanings in this context: that which is temporally prior; that which is ontologically prior (that is, it must necessarily exist before something else can logically exist); and that which is prior in meaning and value. Temporal priority is the least significant aspect of the question. One can argue that time itself is a creation, and therefore the question of temporal priority is not a valid one. The question of ontological priority is more serious, because it asks us to choose which is real, heaven or earth (including our own creations). If heaven is assigned ontological priority, then our world is reduced to a shadowy reflection of a more real domain. If the earth is granted ontological priority, then heaven is merely a projection of our values.

The question of priority in meaning and value raises another question: Are there eternal forms in heaven that serve as the source of all our ideas and our creations, or are we the sole arbiters of standards of beauty, goodness, and justice? When we set out to write a book, we devise a plan, or outline. In doing so we see ourselves as creators of reality rather than its discoverers. The ideas must arise from within ourselves, not from "out there." This process suggests that the earth was created before heaven. We must think through everything, because there is no external source for inspiration. But if we forget the plan and allow ourselves to discover a pattern, rather than attempting a deliberate creation, we are led to conclude that heaven was created before the earth. The talmudic response that both were created at the same time allows us to be co-creators while simultaneously affirming that real standards exist independently of our values.

A basic fear, then, connected with our creativity is that what we create—our art—is not related to what is real. However, on closer examination, we discover that creativity is a process of coming into relationship with reality (the same process I have previously ascribed, not coincidentally, to the concept "spirituality").[6] Therefore we cannot say, "art is that which is *not* nature" or "art is opposed to nature," statements reflecting our fear that our creations are not grounded in reality. If nature is reality, then true art cannot be opposed to it. Instead, art serves to focus and highlight nature, making nature's essence more apparent. The artist does not create in order to escape the world but to embrace it more closely and experience it more fully. For example, a mathematician attempting to prove Euler's last theorem is not seeking to manipulate the world. Instead, she is trying to reach another perspective from which to view and celebrate the world. (Of course, not all artists regard their art in this manner. Some believe they are creating *de novo*, not simply releasing "the form encased in the marble.")

If artists are creating new perspectives from which to view existing reality, they are essentially revealing what is already there. What, then, is creativity? Creativity is found, not in the artist's product, but in the process by which the artist is transformed. Creativity is a transformative way.

Genuine creativity is the infusion of the divine. To be truly creative is to open oneself to enthusiasm, to passionate appreciation of life and nature—to open oneself to the transcendental. That creativity brings us in contact with the divine can be seen in the creativity that allows us to discern "laws" of science. The scientist who rediscovers the fact that many separate phenomena can be taken as instances of a single law may be drawn to the gate of wonder. The poet who suddenly finds the right word, that magnificent confluence of meaning and sound, may be drawn to the gate of spirituality. In these instances, the scientist and poet become focused, not on their own creations, but on beauty itself. Our actions and interactions in the world bring us, at times, in touch with something more enduring than the particular event, object, or choice we are dealing with.

Creativity and Terror

Still the terror remains. Those who have seriously tried to create know the paralyzing effect of the blank page or the empty canvas. It is a fear mixed with excitement—a magnificent adventure is about to begin— but still a terror, nevertheless. Perhaps it was an awareness of the fear and a desire to contain it that led the talmudists to raise questions about creation and list the elements necessary for understanding it. "By ten things was the world created: wisdom, understanding, reason, strength, rebuke, might, righteousness, judgment, lovingkindness, compassion."[7] We must explore what this statement means and verify it in terms of our own creative processes.

What might seem at first glance like a mere piling up of qualities is, in fact, a list of carefully discriminated elements. *Wisdom,* for example, is not the same as *understanding,* nor is it equivalent to *reason.* Wisdom is experiential and incorporates all of our self in the knowing. It consists of deep insights into experience. Understanding is not entirely experiential in nature. It is more fully cognitive. Reason, the most cognitive element of the three, leaves experience behind. The distinction between wisdom and reason has been drawn in many religious traditions, as evinced by the writings of the Christian desert fathers and the scriptures of Buddhism, as well as the talmudic statement above. As reason is modified by experience, it becomes understanding. As "the head moves into the heart," understanding becomes wisdom. The metaphor of "the head moving into the heart" is often encountered in religious writing. Western thought has repeatedly separated reason from the emotions, the head from the heart. Periodically, a great teacher emerges and attempts to reunite these two elements, because the split is theoretically fraught with problems and experientially disastrous. The union of head and heart is precisely what is meant by wisdom. When "to know" no longer signifies merely "to have mastery over" or "to have expertise," but includes "to love," reason has been transformed into wisdom.

Creation requires *strength*, the next item on the list, both to shape recalcitrant matter and to continue creating after we have failed. It is not enough to face the blank page once. Day after day we must return to it and to the mountains of discarded pages. It is said that God did not create the world once for all time but renews the work of creation every day.[8] We know from our own experience that creation requires such ongoingness, such strength. In analyzing this aspect of creation, we find that the Noah Paradox is at its core. If time makes us weary, does God grow weary as well? The account of the Flood in Genesis seems to suggest just that. Though the world is constantly renewed, God sees it fall further and further from the ideal and finally decides to destroy, rather than create.

The criterion of strength brings us face to face with our ambivalence before creation. There are times when we are tempted to destroy our creations. But the Flood was not simply destruction, it was also re-creation: a severe cutting away of what had been, but with that which was of value supported and sustained in the ark, which represents creation floating atop destruction. Creation was not negated in the Flood. The rituals and ceremonies, such as seedtime and harvest, remain. Also remaining is the principle that the act of reproduction has been passed on to the creatures. Whatever else was negated in the Flood, our role as co-creator remains.

Rebuke has two meanings in the context of the talmudic list: that we can accept rebuke and that we can

rebuke ourselves. Creation is not just fecundity. It requires discrimination, discernment, correction, and, at
times, rejection. The latter has one meaning when we
are the creator but quite another when we are the
creature. We know we are flawed and that we do not
live up to the ideal envisioned by the Creator. We wonder
what form the rebuke for our imperfections will take.
Think how we react to our own flawed creations. Sometimes we patch them up or rework them, but other
times we destroy them in disgust. Such thoughts, while
frightening, bring into sharp focus a central story in
Genesis, referred to in Jewish tradition as the *Akedah*,
or "binding" of Isaac. Abraham hears the voice of God
commanding him to take his only son, Isaac, "whom
he loves," to Mount Moriah and offer him as a sacrifice.
Abraham acts without saying a word. He takes Isaac to
the mountain, but at the crucial moment the voice of
God calls out to Abraham to stay his hand: the sacrifice
is not wanted. Abraham looks around, discovers a ram
caught in a thicket, and substitutes the ram for Isaac.
Since it was first written down, the story has been
retold, chewed over, interpreted, and reinterpreted many
times.

In thinking about our creativity and the deep ambivalence we feel toward our creations, we can see that
the *Akedah* suggests that we are Abraham. At the same
time we are forced to recognize that the possessive
pronoun *our* cannot be applied to creatures, for they do
not belong to us. And if we seriously consider the idea
of separation in the Creation story, we realize that
creations do not even belong to God. They belong to
themselves.

Might is the power that creation both needs and
generates. Might refers not to our own reluctant will
(which requires strength to act) but to the creative forces.
We cannot summon might or control it, because it passes
through us, but we can obstruct or distort it. Behind

the concept of might is the mystery that connects our creativity to its source.

Righteousness requires us not to create if we are unwilling to let our creations take on independent life. If we wish merely to churn out predictable artifacts, then we manufacture, not create. Genuine creation requires that we relinquish some of our own power so that the creature can become itself. If we are not righteous, if we do not give the creation its independence, we should not create. Righteousness brings to the fore a central element of the Noah Paradox, that of creation gone awry, as it did at the time of the Flood. Despite such problems, we, like God, create and then respect the otherness of our creations.

Judgment of good and evil, of constraint, and of fittingness is essential to the creative process. Creation does not result from spontaneous inspiration, it is executed with great care. Like the other criteria, judgment reminds us of our flawed nature and leaves us troubled about judging, given our own unworthiness.

As if in response to this concern about our unworthiness, the rabbis end the list with the two attributes that lie at the heart of creation: *loving-kindness* and *compassion*. Creation is an act of love; we create out of fullness. Some have argued that we sometimes create as a response to pain. However, it is not pain itself but our refusal to be defeated by it that leads us to create. We create because we love, and we remain in loving relationship with our creations while restraining our impulse to control them.

By giving us the list of the ten elements of creation, the rabbis help us understand our own creative processes and, at the same time, help us relate our creativity to God's. The gain in understanding defuses the terror associated with creation.

The Beginning of an Idea

We return now to Genesis, not to discover God's creative process, but to understand our own. "When God began to create." What does it mean to *begin*? For example, can we trace a thought to its inception? A group of fourth- and fifth-century desert monks attempted to do so in examining temptation, or evil thought, and discerned six progressive stages:

1. *provocation*, the initial impulse, an image-free stimulation of the heart;
2. *momentary disturbance* of the intellect (What was that sensation, anyway?);
3. *communion*, or coupling, in which we begin to "entertain" the idea, turning it over in our mind as it becomes a thought;
4. *assent*, in which we resolve to act on the thought;
5. *prepossession*, the stage in which the thought becomes a building block in a whole structure made up of habits; and
6. *passion*, or total engagement.[9]

We can follow the movement from an impulse to a disturbance to an idea to a thought to a resolution to act and finally to a state in which the thought becomes part of us. If we examine the stages of thought carefully, we find that they mirror the steps of the Creation as detailed in Genesis 1.

The first stage, image-free stimulation of the heart, corresponds to the condition of *tohu* and *bohu*, the chaos and void or the nothingness that is the source of creative energy. Stage one is prelinguistic—it cannot be talked about—so we use the designation "nothingness," which is not to be understood conceptually but is to be taken as a phenomenological description. All is promise, all is potential, but as yet we have only the energy, undirected and value-free. Eventually, out of that mystery, impulses arise. The image-free stimulation touches the intellect, giving us something to think about, hence, something that must be named: "And God said, 'Let there be light.'" Having named the thought, we are free to toy with it, turning it every which way to explore its potentialities: "And God separated the light from the darkness. God called the light day, and the darkness he called night." God assents to the Creation by calling it "good" (the fourth stage) and the creation of light and darkness becomes the building block (the fifth stage) for the remaining days of Creation. The final stage postulated by the desert fathers is that of passion or total engagement. There is no question about whether God is fully engaged with Creation.

Examining our creativity brings us insights into our relationship with God, but it raises some serious problems as well. We observe a curious dance of creation and destruction. There is bringing forth and there is pruning back. We discover the need for righteousness to allow the creation to take on its own life. And we feel the anguish caused by creation gone awry. Underlying everything is the passionate, ongoing engagement that the desert fathers allude to. Yet can we be so engaged and still be righteous?

We have seen that creativity requires courage. There are dangers inherent in creating something new. Nevertheless, we enter into nothingness and painstakingly bring forth the insights dwelling in this fruitful darkness.

3. Noah's Flood and Ezekiel's Rainbow

As difficult and demanding as creation is, it is less difficult than re-creation. It is only *after* creation, after the devastation brought on by our judgment that creation has gone awry, that we must deal with the Noah Paradox. In the face of destruction and aware of our fallibility, we are asked to build anew, or re-create.

Periodically, we are forced to experience the terrors of a Flood, a shattering of the very foundations of our world. One such Flood for the Children of Israel was the siege of Jerusalem, resulting in the destruction of the Temple and the exile to Babylon.

> Jerusalem has greatly sinned, therefore she is become a mockery. All who admired her despise her, for they have seen her disgraced; and she can only sigh and shrink back. Her uncleanness clings to her skirts. She gave no thought to her future; she has sunk appallingly, with none to comfort her. (Lam. 1:8–9)

In this context, Ezekiel has his first vision. The Children of Israel are already in exile, and he warns that soon Jerusalem will be taken and the Temple destroyed. Recognizing the love and goodness inherent in our initial creation is not enough to sustain us under such an assault. God loved us at our creation, but too much has occurred since. We feel that perhaps we are no longer loved. Ezekiel's vision should be interpreted as a response to this kind of rupture of one's relationship with God.

The Bow That Shines in the Clouds

The text of Ezekiel describes a vision of a stormy wind "sweeping out of the north—a huge cloud and flashing fire, surrounded by a radiance; and in the center of it, in the center of the fire, a gleam as of amber." Then come "the figures of four creatures," followed by a description of the wheels within wheels and "an awe-inspiring gleam as of crystal" above the heads of the creatures. The surrounding radiance is "like the appearance of the bow which shines in the cloud on the day of rain" (Ezek. 1:4–28). The comparison brings us back to God's covenant

> that never again shall the waters become a Deluge, to bring all flesh to ruin! When the bow is in the clouds I will look at it, to call to mind the age-old covenant between God and all living beings—all flesh that is upon the earth. God said to Noah: This is the sign of the covenant that I have established between me and all flesh that is upon the earth. (Gen. 9:15–17)

God's covenant brings us back to the Noah Paradox.

According to Hagigah (a section of the Talmud), Ezekiel's vision should not be studied. The rabbis debated how much of the book of Ezekiel might be taught, and they recounted tales of what happened to young students who unwisely studied the forbidden passages. Ezekiel's vision was considered dangerous for the unprepared scholar.

No matter what we can make of wheels within wheels and four-headed angels, we do know something about rainbows. We know that a rainbow is ephemeral and rather faint, and that a change of perspective can render it invisible to us. Yet this weak and transitory apparition must carry the weight of symbolizing our first covenant with God. Both the rainbow's evanescent nature and our perception of it constitute the danger in studying the Ezekiel text. We are accustomed to thinking of religion as something that has always existed and that we receive by being born into it. But in Ezekiel we are asked to reconceive religion as something transitory. Like the rainbow, it must continue to bear the weight of symbolizing the convenant. And at the same time, it is dependent upon *our* perspective, that is, our ability to perceive and interpret it. We want religion to support us, to carry the full weight of meaning and value, and to sustain our world. But Ezekiel's vision suggests that it is we who must support religion, by conceiving and perceiving the world so that it can hold meaning and nourish future generations.

It is frightening to realize that our world is made of the fragile elements of love, commitment, and faith and that if we change our perspective, we may cease to experience the brightness and color of our world. Yet within that fragile structure, we find all that is needed to nourish us spiritually.

Losing Faith

Suppose we have been living a life of love, commitment, and faith. We feel safe enough to ask challenging questions, such as: Did the Torah really come down to us at Mount Sinai? Can you really love me and still be so critical of my family? It is surprising how strong and resilient our world is when tested from within, much as an eggshell is strong when pressure is applied to either end. But suddenly and unwillingly, we may find ourselves outside what had been our world, no longer tied by the bonds of love, commitment, and faith. As one person who lost faith put it, "After years of praying I realized I had only been talking to myself." How fragile that world now appears when viewed from outside, and how easy to see its faults and destroy it, like squeezing the eggshell in the middle, where it is weak.

If we have lived our lives within the protective doctrines of a religion, only to awaken one day outside the faith, our reactions are likely to be confused. We might pretend that we are not outside the faith and go through all the rituals, without acknowledging that we have lost our inner faith. We might consider faith a childhood fantasy and call our new status maturity. We might rail at the doctrine, for having been deceptive and seek to convince others of its insubstantiality. Or, we might simply bemoan our loss of belief, faith, and optimism, feeling that their loss is the natural byproduct of aging. Religious faith is easily destroyed, because it is made up of such fragile elements as wonder, love, and commitment. All too frequently, these elements are destroyed by us in anger, disappointment, or sadness.

Reconstructing the Rainbow

Ezekiel's vision suggests that our task after losing faith is to construct a new rainbow in order to re-create faith, a task we will come to see as life-sustaining. If we remember our earlier belief and trust, we can use the experience, which was neither delusional nor insubstantial, to teach us how to re-create our faith. We lose faith not because of weak belief, poor teaching, or any fallen nature. We *must* wake up outside our inherited faith, so that we can create a new faith to replace the one we merely inherited. Our first faith nourished us and allowed us to grow, but ultimately *we* must build our own faith. Now we are beginning to recognize that there is an active role we must play in resolving the Noah Paradox. The rainbow reminds us that our job is to reconstruct this world. We are not to destroy it, although we may want to *de-construct* it, that is, take it apart piece by piece to see what it consists of.

We enter into the unknown world of lack of faith and attempt to bring forth insight from the darkness. Once we recognize that we are also makers of faith and meaning, we must ask what aspects of ourselves we should bring to this task. Commitment is not the product of pure cognition. No amount of rational thought can bring us to the domain of meaning and value. We turn instead to our imagination, which represents the boundary connecting the external world with what is within us. Our new faith, like the rainbow, results not only from our seeing sunlight refracted through drops of moisture but also from our imaginative interpretation of hope and our recollection of God's covenant with us.

We must each discover our own way to God. We cannot know God simply by being obedient, that is, by following the teachings of our parents or institutionalized religion. At some point, we must make the creative leap.

Creativity

Creativity allows us to experience and express transcendent love. We create relationships, systems of meaning, forms of expression, nourishing and protective environments, and offspring who will carry on the creative process. We create systems of justice, political institutions, and ways of overcoming misery. In each of our creations, we incorporate the creativity we experience in the cosmos. In other words, creativity is grounded in spirituality, that is, in coming into relationship with reality. For example, we are driven to create relationships by a sense of relatedness that precedes our creation: we have been loved, and we pass on the gift of love. We find the world meaningful, so we create systems of meaning. The world supports us with its air, water, warmth, and food, and in turn, we create our own shelter and comfort. The world appears to be the expression of its Creator's love and concern, so we too create out of love. We were given the gift of life, and we pass on that gift by having children. We find the natural world lawful, so we create legal systems. We have experienced interconnections in creation, so we try to model our political institutions so they will foster and nourish our own interconnectedness. We sense the care and protection that sustains the weaker aspects of creation, so we find ourselves caring for the powerless and voiceless. And we have found comfort and a healing of our suffering in creation, so we strive to comfort, heal, and mend the world. In studying our creative processes, we realize that the creative life is identical with the spiritual life.

The call to create is troubling. Earlier, when we attempted to understand God's creation from within our own creativity, we had to face our ambivalence about being creative. Ezekiel's warning of the impending destruction of Jerusalem and the Temple is a call to examine our own creativity, a difficult task. The siege of Jerusalem, the Babylonian exile, and the impending destruction of the Temple were as catastrophic as the Flood. Ezekiel's vision counters the Flood with the call to create. Our call is to be aware of this moment of impending destruction and, within this context, to create a new radiance. We must re-create after our world falls apart.

Four Steps to Creativity

Writers on creativity have called the first step in the creative process, *preparation*. This step corresponds to what is described above as "living within the radiance." We are born and raised in a religious tradition that teaches us the basic symbols, language, and questions of that tradition. Exile, war, and the razing of the Temple have destroyed important symbols of our faith. We must rebuild. But if there had been no destruction, we would have to rebuild anyway. We cannot live without questioning our received tradition if our creative spirit is to function. When our inherited images no longer hold for us, we must be willing to let go even if it means entering darkness and chaos. In either case—the destruction of our world by outside forces or the erosion from within us—we feel genuine loss, pain, and suffering. Destruction by external forces may appear to be the severe pruning of "rebuke": Has God wearied of this wayward creation? If the change is from within us, it feels like a response to a deeper call for authenticity, yet we do not let go of cherished symbols without a sense of guilt. The earlier tradition had nurtured us, so are we justified in shattering it?

This painful period of tearing away, sundering, and destruction leads to the second stage in the creative process, *incubation*. The creative process, at this stage, demands that we relinquish control so that the new perspective can begin to grow. We let go of all we have learned, all that has given structure and security to our lives, and experience a time of fear and danger. We don't know what to believe, how to pray, how to understand the fundamental human experiences. The learned responses of our former faith are no longer there to guide us as we face suffering, loss, solitude, and confusion. We cannot act, we lose control, and we endure wrenching feelings and disorientation. Our entry into this chaos, or darkness, may not even be deliberate. While we can sometimes empty ourselves of received images through reflection, more often we are emptied through pain and despair. The seemingly secure world that the images provide can collapse through loss. It is less often true that we let go of the images than that they cannot support the weight of reality. This happens with children whose earliest idea of God includes the notion of God as protector of the innocent. When a young friend dies they frequently lose not only the friend, but their idea of God. This time of chaos and disorientation is frequently called "darkness." As we have already seen, darkness traditionally has a negative connotation, but in the process of reconstructing the rainbow, we must embrace the insights of prophets and mystics concerning the positive values of darkness. The darkness of our creative process can be understood on three related levels: first, that which cannot be understood (for example, the knowledge of ignorance); second, that which cannot be imagined; and third, that which entails pain and suffering.

Most of us are aware that there are things we do not know and cannot ever know. In admitting this, we may feel shame or think that we should have greater mastery over the world. We see our ignorance as a type of darkness. In the story of the Exodus, Pharoah experiences darkness as the next-to-last plague. The darkness is literal darkness, absence of light, but it is also the darkness of a reversal of values, typified by all the plagues. In the first plague, the Nile, which had been the source of fertility, is changed into a river of putrification. Pharaoh, as a deity, is supposed to protect his peoples' livestock and crops. Instead, he becomes the cause of cattle disease and locust infestation. Each plague challenges his conception of the world, but he refuses to deal with the challenge. The darkness of the second stage of creation shows us that we grow by realizing our ignorance: knowing the limits of what we *can* know enables us to learn better, to correct, and to be corrected. His experience of darkness did not shake Pharoah's view of the world, but we can allow our world to be shattered and creatively restructured by acknowledging the darkness that surrounds our experience of light.

The second level of darkness is that which cannot be imagined. The biblical injunction against making graven images of what cannot be imagined brings out the difference between appearance and reality. We cannot engrave, fix in stone, our present perception of reality. It teaches us to continue to look for the deeper reality: the tattered beggar may actually be a saint. The commandment against graven images is more than just an injuction against representing God. Because we are created in the image of God, the commandment forbids us to make images of ourselves as well. We can understand the importance of this law by considering that the opposite of an image is reality. If we reverse the injunction against making images, we obtain the positive commandment to be real, genuine, and authentic. We all have images of ourselves, and it is hard to let go of them and simply be ourselves. We picture who we are supposed to be and then convince ourselves that that is who we are. But rather than picture ourselves, we should *be* ourselves and experience who we truly are.

The darkness of pain and suffering results not from sin but from the full extent of our love. Rabbi Akiba, the second-century teacher, severed the nexus between suffering and retribution. He held that "suffering is precious" and did not interpret it as a result of justice. In his opinion, "compassion does not enter into judgment." For him, suffering does not come as a consequence of justice, but as a product of love. The disproportion between us and the transcendent object of our love causes the pain of stretching out and reaching for the infinite. While our love may cause us pain, it is not a masochistic effort, but rather a determination to grow. If we focus on the determination to grow, the concomitant pain will be as unremarkable as the pain a dancer feels during a ballet performance or a marathon runner feels during the strenuous push to the finish line.

The three forms of darkness we have discussed—that which cannot be understood, that which cannot be imaged, and that which entails pain—are essential aspects of the creative process. We enter into these forms of darkness whenever we fully enter into a relationship. If the process of entering a relationship is the creative process, then love must be the source of creativity and is itself the deepest creative act. The otherness of the partner in the relationship prevents us from fully knowing or controlling the relationship. Neither can we portray the relationship; its shape eludes us. Frequently, it stretches and tempers us, wearing away our harsher edges. While it is experientially clear that relationships entail pain and suffering, it is not spiritually clear why this should be. If the pain of the spiritual quest comes from the disproportion between the finite and the infinite, what accounts for the suffering caused by relationships between two people? The answer is the same— a disproportion between the finite and the infinite— because in a relationship, we love in another person the particular aspect that opens out onto the infinite (loving another as a finite or limited being would reduce the person to an object). By recognizing the loved one as an infinite mystery, we revere the aspect of the other person that is unlimited.

The third stage in the creative process, *illumination*, occurs after we stop faithfully accepting the doctrines and teachings of others and reach beyond the evidence before us. Our knowledge comes not from any external source or authority but from our experience. Such direct, experiential knowledge transforms us through its immediacy and leads us to what constitutes the final stage of the creative way, *verification*, in which we feel an urge to complete our work. Experiential knowledge—insight that grows out of our being—drives us to act in terms of that knowledge.

The call to rebuild the rainbow is a lonely one that takes us into darkness. Regardless of how many have come along the same path, our journey is unique, because experiential insight must be individually perceived and comprehended. The action that results from our findings is unique to each individual, just as the discovery itself is, but it always furthers the work we are called upon to do.

Creativity and Spirituality

All we can say about the stages leading to the creative experience is true as well of the spiritual quest—that is, we can prepare the ground, and we can wait. Neither experience can be obtained simply by will. The experience of presence, or grace, is either given or not given, and the creative moment either comes or does not come. The similarity of the two experiences is essential, not accidental. Grace is not one thing and creativity another with certain significant resemblances. Creativity *is* grace, a gift of presence. In creative moments we are touched by the Divine Presence: "Singers and dancers alike will say/'All my roots are in You'" (Ps. 87:7).

Religious life is problematic. We may move from a relatively simple spiritual existence within the structures of shared images and forms of worship to find ourselves outside these familiar structures and forms. We may have left because the images were too patriarchal or too hierarchical, but usually the causes behind the change elude such simple analysis. We were in the light, and yet we found a strong force pulling us toward the darkness. The patterns that mark our religious life mark our creative life as well. Our prayers, once sweet with "consolations," turn arid, but we can't return to our earlier way of prayer. Our creative life once flowed, effortlessly, with fresh insights. Now we plough the ground, sharpen our pencils, and suffer through long periods during which we create nothing. In these cases, we may be moving from one kind of religious or creative life to another. The freshness of the new insight can be achieved only after we have experienced the chaos of the time outside our familiar and consoling patterns. The freshness will return, but only after we have come through the darkness.

Ezekiel's vision affirms that, in answer to a Flood, we must re-create. Ezekiel acknowledges the difficulties in re-creating after destruction, but the imperative remains. In creating we move beyond the Noah Paradox and meet the Creator.

4. Another Flood: Destruction of the Temple and the Vision of the New Jerusalem

Ezekiel's first vision preceded the fall of Jerusalem and the destruction of the Temple. It was a call to the Israelites to re-envision their faith in a way that would let them accept these disasters and yet go on living. Ezekiel's final vision occurs "in the twenty-fifth year of our exile" (Ezek. 40:1), a statement that both locates the people in time and recalls to them their tremendous loss. By this time his prophecy had come true: Jerusalem had fallen and the Temple had been destroyed. The destruction of the Temple was not simply the loss of a magnificent building, it was the end of an entire way of worship. In this period, Jewish worship centered on the daily offerings in the Temple. Sacrifice was permitted only in the Temple, and prayer and study had not yet become the dominant modes of worship. Losing the Temple meant losing the only path to God's presence for most Jews of the time. Through a vision Ezekiel is brought to the Land of Israel, to the high mountain of Isaiah and Micah, to the Temple area. He measures off the wall around the Temple, the threshold of the gate, the recesses, and the inner vestibule of the gate.

Then Ezekiel is taken to the outer court, where he measures all the gates, then into the inner court, and then into the great hall. Everywhere he measures the walls, the depth, the entrance. Is Ezekiel drawing up a blueprint for reconstructing the Temple? Certainly in

51

exile it is natural to dream of home, to recall all the sights on the homeward route, and to remember how many steps it takes to reach familiar landmarks. So Ezekiel's vision could be interpreted as forward looking, as a blueprint for rebuilding the Temple. Or, it could be understood as an exercise in nostalgia: after twenty-five years in exile, he still dreams longingly of the glory that once was.

But if the Temple itself symbolizes a deeper reality, then a vision of the Temple probably symbolizes not the physical structure but the reality behind the Temple. What *was* the Temple? What *is* the Temple? And why build one at all?

The Temple in Jerusalem (*Mikdash* in Hebrew) was the center of worship in Judaism. It grew out of the meeting tent (*mishkan*) used by the Children of Israel in the wilderness. The chance encounters with God in the desert were thus given a locus, first in the meeting tent and later in the Temple. The Temple was the place where the Israelites met the Holy, and in our times the Temple still represents the place where we meet the Holy.

All of us have lived through the destruction of a Temple, that is, some place where we have been able (perhaps only on rare occasions) to experience the presence of God. The Temple for many of us is our family, where in quiet moments we suddenly feel an all-enveloping love. Then our family configuration changes. Perhaps the children grow up and decide to move away. The occasion is one for rejoicing, but we also feel a strong sense of loss. The years spent with the children have left us unprepared for their departure. Will we still be able to find God in the quiet moments at home without them? Or perhaps we have lost a spouse through divorce or death. Once, the marriage may have represented a covenant to us, but the marriage is no more. Has the covenant also disappeared? On the other hand, our primary locus for the Holy may not be family, but work. In the workplace, we may meet the Holy in the work itself or through interactions with our colleagues. But workplaces change. Perhaps our colleagues no longer care about the same things, and the work seems less and less a sacred calling. Or, our Temple may be a traditional house of worship, but new people have joined the community, the liturgy has evolved, and it has been a long time since the house of worship has felt like anything more than a social hall.

At such times, two things are needed. First, we must allow ourselves to feel our loss. We could, of course, try to convince ourselves that our prior experiences of the Holy were simply products of a deceitful memory. After all, nostalgia surrounds past events with a happy glow. Maybe we never did feel the Holy when the children were home. It was all so busy and noisy that we couldn't really have had those quiet moments of transcendence, could we? If our marriage no longer *is*, then in some sense it probably never *was*. Using this tactic, we rewrite our past to write out the numinous moments. But if we wish to reestablish contact with God, we must admit that there *was* a Temple. Only in remembering and mourning it can we begin the process of recovering it. The second thing we need is hope that we will succeed in finding the Holy again. We know that the Holy is real; we have experienced it. If a new place and a mode of meeting are required, then we will build a new Temple, one flowing with living water.

But what will serve as our blueprint? If our Temple is supposed to be a microcosm of creation as a whole, then we should look to the creation of the world for a plan. Our other choice is to look within ourselves, because the structures of our own consciousness are the structures of the Temple. Two answers, one Temple, but we need not choose between the answers, because both are correct. There is a significant confluence between the structures of creation and the structures of our mind.

A Vision of the Temple as a Vision of Creation

We can analyze Ezekiel 40 in terms of the Creation account in Genesis 1. The text of Ezekiel reveals a pervasive concern about separation. For example, we read that the massive wall enclosing the Temple area was not erected for the sake of fortification but for separating the holy area from its secular surroundings. "It seems likely that the emphasis upon the verb 'to separate' (*hivdil*) here [in the description of the new Temple] is intended to suggest the primordial acts of separation that punctuate the act of creation (Gen. 1:4, 6, 7, 14, 18). . . . [The building of the Temple serves as a] perpetuation of the very process that brought order out of chaos."[1] The act of separating, a major part of the original creation, plays an analogous role in the creation of the new Temple. So do the other steps of Creation mentioned in Genesis: emptiness, openness, waiting, calling forth, seeing, evaluating, naming, limiting, placing, marking of time, blessing and releasing of the creatures' own creativity, creating in the Creator's own image, and ceasing to create.

We can find another blueprint for building a Temple that is modeled on the Creation by looking at several properties of creatures. The first of these properties is *origin*.[2] We can look at anything and ask: Why is there *something* and not nothing? But when we explore the origin of a creature we come face to face with our own contingency and mortality. Our essence does not entail existence. We can easily be conceived of as not existing. Indeed, there was a time before we existed and there will be a time after. This reflection shows our radical dependency: without God we would not be, and, more importantly, we would not have meaning. We will die, and to some extent we have to come to terms with that. There are even causes we may be willing to die for. But our death itself occurs within an enduring system of meaning: a lasting framework of relationships we have been part of, values that we have espoused, and communities to which we have contributed. Without this system of meaning, we would be dead in a far more absolute sense: our being would cease to be distinct from our nonbeing, and nothing would persist, perdure, or matter. There must be some essence that takes up and preserves the distinctions around which we form our lives. Let us look at origin, then, in terms of our own creativity. "An original idea is a revelation of [God], bringing something from nothingness to existence. At first you do not know the idea at all. It still exists within the Infinite in a state of nothingness. This is the source of all wisdom. Every new idea is drawn from this source. We therefore see [God's] revelation in each new idea."[3] Facing the emptiness and uncertainty is a way of meeting God. Our daily struggle with the blank paper is not to draw something beautiful or to make a name for ourselves, but a way of forming a relationship with God. Our daily confrontation with emptiness represents our continual willingness to experience the Origin of all origins and to find in origination a locus of the Holy.

The first property of creatures points to our confrontation with the abyss, nothingness, nonbeing, and nonmeaning. We are tempted to draw back, but the second property, *magnitude*, brings us back to the physical world from the spiritual one. Magnitude simply means that the creation is enormous, even overwhelming, in its spaciousness. At night we can lie on our backs and view the visible stars; beyond them, stars we only half see, and beyond them, stars we can only imagine. The creation is infinite, and the thought fills us with wonder. The universe is not only infinite in size, it is infinite in its complexity and in the interconnectedness and multiplicity of life forms it supports. For example, a tree is much like a city. It is the locus of life for many different creatures. Birds live in its higher branches, squirrels lower down, insects in and around its bark, and lichens grow near the roots. Each of its inhabitants carries within itself worlds of life, from the microorganisms living with the lichen to the many cells of the squirrel's body. The property illustrated by the tree and its inhabitants is *multitude*. Magnitude reminds us that the creative surge is powerful, and we feel afraid because we cannot control it. It is a gift. One can either block the gift or be prepared for it. Multitude reminds us that the creative surge also has intricate associations.

We now must deal with another property of creation, *beauty*. Why is the world so beautiful? It would function as well physically if it were drab. That is because beauty is not functional, it is a gift of grace. Creation is not an indifferent bringing forth, it is a gift of love. There is beauty not only in the Creation but in our creations as well. There are moments when we look at what we have created and discover that it is beautiful. The beauty in our creation is less something we have deliberately produced than something we discover after the fact. Our creations therefore seem to be related to Creation. Even as we act to create, we are also receiving.

Still another property of creation is *fullness*. Fullness refers to the deep satisfaction the world offers. When we look at our creations, we sometimes feel a sense of satiety, "of making books there is no end, and much study is a weariness of the flesh" (Eccles. 12:12). In contrast, the world is inexhaustible. There are layers and layers of richness and delight. And our own creativity must emulate this fullness. If we have something worthwhile to say, we should say it. The more we spend, the more we will have. We cannot afford to save something for another book. But fullness means more than giving all we have. It refers to the sense of expansiveness we experience as we pour ourselves into our creation. We withhold nothing and receive everything.

As we look at creation, we become aware that creation is *active*. Activity means that things exist (are *actual*) and that they have motion and energy. Creation is a dynamic process. The world is alive, vibrant, and overflowing. This property of creatures and of our creations most closely mirrors who we are and what we are to become. We want to be fully alive, growing and contributing, fully conscious and caring. Our creating actualizes the person we were meant to be.

The final property of creatures we will discuss, *order*, expresses the essential realization that Creation is ordered and structured: it all fits together and forms a meaningful whole. What is true of creation must be true of our creativity as well. "Without our own contribution we see nothing."[4] The realization of how much we contribute to the world does not negate this world, but it does make clear to what extent the world is made up of our sensibilities. The seven properties of creation that we named—origin, magnitude, multitude, beauty, fullness, activity, and order—were first listed by Bonaventure. Each of these properties describes creatures, and each applies as well to our vision of the new Temple, which symbolizes both our structures of consciousness and the place where we meet the Divine Presence. The properties apply to the new Temple, and like the new Temple, each is a creative tool that can be used to rebuild a locus for holiness.

Failure and Re-Creation

If we look to God's Creation as a blueprint for our re-creation of the Temple, we must recognize that one of the elements built into the notion of creation is the

sequence of failure, backsliding, and re-creation. Creation does not end with Genesis 2:4. It includes the
destruction and re-creation found in the story of Noah.
It also includes the calling of Abraham. It extends
beyond Genesis, because God renews the work of creation every day. In that sense, Creation extends into
the present. But our sense of God's unique Creation
recedes as we become more and more a party to the
ongoing process of creation.

Our role in creation is a way of explaining the traditional view that the Torah is not in heaven but in
our heart and in our mouth. We are accepting responsibility for our role in creation. We can look at our
creative role in terms of the special creative enterprise
of parenting. First there is the initial creation, birth.
Next comes all the shaping involved in teaching, train-
ing, and living in a family. Then there is the new role
of being the parents of an adult child. To what extent
are the parents of an adult child still creating? As the
child grows older, the messages the parents tried to
instill become more accessible to the child, but the
parents are not giving new messages. The parents must
finally trust that what they once taught the child is
somehow buried deep within the child, and while it is
now covered over with many new ideas and values, it
will ultimately show itself.

In an analogous way, God is there in our formation
and liberation, and in our revelation. The way to God
remains open, but God will not speak again at Sinai.
What was taught once will not be repeated. We must
learn it without God's help. Just as our children come
to understand who we are and what we have given
them once they become parents, so, as we create, we
begin to understand God and God's creation. We understand the necessity of letting go and the pain involved. We understand the fear that our creation does
not have adequate safeguards. We fear that we, too, will

have to destroy our creation with a flood. We wonder if we can more intimately and directly create, in the way that God worked with Abraham and Noah.

A Vision of the Temple as a Vision of Our Consciousness

Creation is an important blueprint for rebuilding the Temple, but it is not the only one. The second blueprint for the Temple is in terms of the components of our mind. Bonaventure portrays the journey through the Temple (and our mind) as moving from the outer court of sensation to the sanctuary (the forward area of the tabernacle) where the light burns (the light of truth), until he reaches the Holy of Holies.[5] Bonaventure's description of our mind is rich, but Ezekiel's is richer still, with additional distinctions and an inner court. Also, there are aspects of our psychology not delineated in Bonaventure's description. Essentially, Bonaventure describes three levels of the self: *sensation*, which is relegated to the outer court and brings the outer world into the inner; *reason*, which can recognize truth and is our inner sense of ourselves; and the *Holy of Holies*, which is located beyond reason in the innermost recesses of consciousness.

The senses are indeed our most exterior aspect, but this outer court of sensation must connect by a passageway to the Holy of Holies. Senses are not merely passive; they are shaped by reason, emotions, sense of self, and creative imagination. As part of the blueprint, we need a realization that the Holy of Holies not only draws in the world but radiates out to it. Practically speaking, what this means is that we sense external stimuli, think about them, and then respond to them. Sensation is not simply the passive reception of stimuli but also the active shaping of impressions of those stimuli.

Our inner court (the faculty of reason) has additional aspects not mentioned by Bonaventure. Besides being the seat of reason, the inner court includes emotions and the three dimensions of memory: the repository of past impressions, the innate ideas we hold in common with all of humanity, and the locus of personal identity that persists through a lifetime of changes. We can, in principle, mentally remain in the inner court, occupied by our familiar sense of self, composed of sensation, reason, emotions, and memory. But we have the chance to open the vestibule to the Holy of Holies. This vestibule is the creative imagination.

Many people block off the creative imagination. It is beyond the self in the sense of ego and is accessible through meditation and ecstasy. Knowledge of the Holy of Holies depends on the power of the imagination. If we try to visualize the structure of the Temple, it will help us to realize why the awakening of the imagination is a sign of redemption. Intellectually we recognize that the awakening of the imagination is a sign of redemption because the imagination gives us the challenge of hope. But when we focus on the Temple structure as a clue, we recognize the redemptive aspect of the imagination, because redemption comes from the experience of the presence of God, an experience open only through the vestibule of the creative imagination. When the vestibule is blocked, there is no access to the Holy of Holies: "Her gates have sunk into the ground; he has ruined and broken her bars; her kings and princes are among the nations; the law is no more, and her prophets obtain no vision from the Lord"[5] (Lam. 2:9). But the resurgence of the imagination informs us that the vestibule is open and that we are being nourished by access to the Holy of Holies. Ezekiel's visionary Temple also shows us that there is an intimate relationship between creativity and

and those who favored adapting the order so that it could expand and develop along institutional lines. These who wanted to follow the ideals of Francis also prophesied an end of Church institutions and a free life of the Spirit. Bonaventure saw the dangers of creative imagination. Creativity is powerful, but the power can be used for either good or evil. We cannot predict what creativity will open us up to. Bonaventure apparently did not want to deal with the dark side of creativity. The biblical stories, for instance, demonstrate that the attempt to force creativity is invariably destructive. The examples in Genesis consistently show this. For example, Leah and Rachel compete to bear Jacob children. At first the competition is based solely on the level of hope and aspiration. But when Leah's son finds mandrakes (an herb thought to aid fertility), Rachel bargains with Leah for them. Leah lets Rachel have them, and it is Leah, not Rachel, who becomes pregnant. Rachel again tries (and fails) to control her fate by stealing her father's teraphim (idols). Her death is usually attributed to Jacob's curse (made to emphasize his own innocence of the theft) that whoever has stolen the teraphim should die. The relationship of creativity and destruction is a persistent theme in Jacob's family: the rape of Dinah and subsequent slaughter of all of the people of Shechem by Simeon and Levi; the death in childbirth of Rachel; the loss of his father's blessing when Reuben sleeps with his father's concubine. All of the acts relate to sexuality and creativity, creativity of deception and retribution.

Destruction is an essential part of creation, a part that is frequently beneficial. We see that when a surgeon cuts away diseased tissue for the sake of saving the rest of the organ. The creative process, like the mystic practice of purgation, causes a type of dying. An aspect of self must die. This type of negative growth can be understood as a cutting away of unwanted accretions picked up in the process of living. But it can also be understood in the positive sense of deliberately under-taking challenges that will cause us to go beyond our-selves and transcend our previous limits.

When we enter into creativity we must let go of the plan, the outline, the calculated outcome. Our job is to *discover* a pattern, not attempt to create one. Even if we are trying to avoid doing so, we can unwittingly fall into a pattern. This is not true creativity, because it does not bring us into the presence of the Holy, but leads us into a deceptive way of thought. That is, it leads us to think that we can control that which is actually a gift. We see this in people who keep painting the same subject. This approach to creativity is safe, because it is dead. Creativity and life both entail risk. If we let go of the pattern, we will be surprised. Crea-tivity is a gift. Only if we recognize and accept and trust the gift can we be authentically creative.

Beyond Nonbeing

In planning our rebuilding of the Temple, we should note that the text of Ezekiel 43 mentions more than just the physical structure. "Then he led me to a gate, the gate that faced east. And there, coming from the east with a roar like the roar of mighty waters, was the Presence of the God of Israel, and the earth was lit up by His Presence" (Ezek. 43:1–2). God's message is to avoid the defiling effect of death in the new construction of the Temple. In the original Temple in Jerusalem there was a common wall shared by the Temple and the palace. When someone died in the palace, the death defiled the whole Temple.

The powerful defiling force of death is due to our nature. We are always torn between nonbeing, the noth-ing out of which we were created, and Being, the image of God after which we were created. Death defiles because we are lured by death. In times of grief or exile we are lured by the temptation of nonbeing. We must fight these temptations. Even in mourning we must focus on releasing what was alive in the one we loved rather than focus on nonbeing. We must concentrate on continuity and ongoingness and not get lost in death. This is an especially urgent message for the twentieth century, a century full of death and destruction. Either we can be frozen by death, turned back to nonbeing, or we can focus on life and how to persevere. That does not mean we should forget the potential for destruction, but it does mean we should focus on the positive alternative. What is important is not that the people we are mourning died, but that they lived. Death did not destroy their essential selves. We remember and revere the lives they lived, not the death that was thrust upon them. But it remains a serious challenge for us. We are drawn to death because of fear, and in the process we relinquish our wonder for life because of our fear of life. "What we lack is not a will to believe but a will to wonder."[8] The pain of loss or of destruction leads us to long for a release from this world and its demands. "As we explore further and further we gradually begin to discover that the Lord is leading us, not into some strange angelic world but deeper and deeper into the heart of our very concrete existence."[9]

Re-Creation and Our Consciousness

The Temple as a model of creation and the Temple as a model of our soul are closely interrelated. We create worlds of meaning and value. And it is in our creative process that we are most deeply made in the image of God. But we have already built temples, and now they lie in ruin before us.

The Temple in Ezekiel's vision can be seen as a "second-order" Temple. Its model is not creation, as the original Tent of Meeting's was, but the Temple. What we are exploring in Ezekiel's vision, then, is not the creation of a Temple, but its *re-creation*. The latter is, in many respects, a more difficult process than creation. As Bernard said, "If I owe all that I am in return for my creation, what am I to add in return for being remade and remade in this way? For I was not remade as easily as I was made."[10] There is a painful difference between creation and re-creation of the Temple, one that is analogous to the difference between the creation of the world and its re-creation after the Flood.

The Flood initiated a new chaos. The foundations of the deep gave way, and the windows of the heavens opened, spilling forth the waters above. Within this chaos of flooding waters remained the ark, retaining the seed of the cosmos in the midst of chaos. Re-creating after a flood is more difficult than creating initially because we are all too aware of the flaws that led to destruction. Re-creation takes place, not with abundant optimism, but with caution. We have many questions. What should we retain from the initial creation? What was right, and what was wrong? What objects should we save and put in the ark? We return to the list of things created in Genesis. Which of those things contained the flaw that led to the Flood and should be left behind? Limit seems essential. It was the absence of limit that allowed the waters to overflow their gates and re-cover the world. Separation, distinction, naming, and evaluating are all necessary. However, consider the blessing and releasing of the creations. This is the step where a flaw can creep in. And yet this is the most important part of creativity. We are made in God's image as creators, and it is in the releasing of our creativity that we enter fully into who we are meant to be. The fulfillment of creativity and the risk of a flaw lie in the same act.

Although Ezekiel's vision chiefly concerns the rebuilding of the Temple, it also includes an awareness of three negative elements: the corruption that occurred before the destruction, the privileged role of priest and Levite, and the presence of alien symbols in this place of holiness. We wonder if it is possible to build a place of holiness that will not ultimately warrant destruction.

As we consider the possibility of constructing our own loci of holiness, we too must face the pain of rebuilding. As God is said to re-create the world daily, we too, perhaps, are required to face anew each day the construction of worlds of meaning and value. Part of re-creation is the retention of that which was of value in the previous creation. Such elements must be carefully preserved in the ark of cosmos that floats over the waters of chaos.[11] But part of re-creating is accepting destruction. There must be a severe pruning of those accretions that have kept us from entering into the experience of the holy.

The Temple was the locus of holiness, the place where people could experience the presence of God. In rebuilding the Temple, we must make *presence* our chief concern, presence that is consciously and deliberately sought and given. Prophecy has usually been thought of as future-oriented: a prophet can predict events that have not yet occurred. That is one meaning of prophecy, but not the most essential one. The prophet's main gift is to see and report the deepest meaning of the *present*. Given this meaning, the prophet Ezekiel's vision of the Temple tells us that God is present *now*.

A major question running throughout the Hebrew Scriptures is, "Is God in our midst?" In other words: Is this right, is this meaningful? This is an especially difficult question for those in exile. Ezekiel 40 responds to that difficulty and can be understood as a description of God's love. Ezekiel talks about the absence of all the external signs of God's love and the way that God's love persists in the midst of the absence. God sought and continues to seek a place where we can meet. "All the developed theology of temples in Israel points to the presence of God as the core of spiritual meaning."[12] Also, "The goal of the exodus is not so much the promised land as it is the intimacy with [God] made available to Israel in the Tabernacle. He rescued her so that He might set up Tent in her midst. The endless rendezvous in the portable temple is the teleological consummation of the history of redemption."[13]

But we have grown careless and seen our place of meeting destroyed. "Under what circumstances can the holy God be present? This is the language of *presence*. Jerusalem is precious because it is where God is present. . . . The gift of life is available only where God's transcendent power is present. Now it is gone, banished in the face of defilement, and where banished, there can only be death. . . . YHWH is known through negative power, known as the one who can be absent, as the one whose glory can depart, whose life-giving power can be withdrawn."

Now we begin to awaken. We seek a way to return to our former relationship. "[There is] the resilient theological optimism which is a hallmark of biblical prophecy and which expresses itself in the (recurrent) possibilities of reconciliation between the sinner and God. . . . The priests also shared an optimistic anthropology and theology of divine-human reconciliation comparable to that which highlights so much of biblical prophecy."[14]

What was at the heart of spiritual meaning in the Temple was the presence of God. But our Temple has been destroyed, and all the rituals that took place in those sacred precincts have fallen into disuse. However, the blueprint for the Temple is contained in the structure of creation and in the structure of our consciousness. In that sense, the Temple has not been destroyed and cannot ever be destroyed. As long as the world exists, we can enter deeply into it and travel the spiritual route from any creature to the creative love that permeates creation. As long as our consciousness exists, we can journey from the world of our senses, through the inner court of reason, emotions, memory, and sense of self, to the vestibule of creative imagination. From there we are summoned to the Holy of Holies.

In conclusion, Ezekiel's vision leads us to explore our creativity, applying the categories of Genesis 1 to our own lives and creative efforts. In so doing, we find standards of meaning and value. We also recognize a source of the Holy. Exploring our creativity and the creativity that surrounds us, we are led to sources of wonder.

But the wonder we discover through our exploration of creativity does not solve all our problems. We must also recognize our responsibility for creating worlds of meaning and value. We had thought that we could live in a world already replete with structures of meaning, only to discover that it is we who must do the structuring. There are temptations to nihilism involved in this realization. But, if we recall the joy of creativity, we will take heart and begin to rebuild.

Beyond the recognition of our responsibility for creation and meaning lies the experience of devastation and loss. Our earlier structures of meaning have not weathered these fierce blasts. Even if family, work, and community have faltered and finally failed to hold up as loci of holiness, a vision remains, a blueprint for rebuilding structures of holiness. Rebuilding is more difficult than the initial building, but it can (and must) be done.

5. Spirituality: Exodus and the Five Stages of the Journey

We have approached the Noah Paradox through the transformative way of creativity. We examined the process of creation and the more problematic process of re-creation. Examining re-creation showed us that creativity does not just produce artifacts, it also has an internal component. Seeing the structural parallels between Ezekiel's visionary Temple and our own consciousness helped us to realize that creativity requires us to enter into our consciousness and to move from the outer courts of sensation, reason, and memory to the vestibule of the Holy of Holies, the creative imagination.

The creative way implies an essential internal transformation; the spiritual way explicitly demands such a program. Internal transformation *is* the spiritual way. Although internal transformation has an external product—changed actions in the world—the emphasis in the spiritual way is on the internal aspects of self-transformation.

Because the spiritual quest concerns mainly intangible internal changes and most people pursue more tangible goals, those involved in the spiritual way often find themselves in need of some guideposts, or standards to validate their uncertain course. To this end, people have used the journey as a framework for discussing these intangible goals. The spiritual journey has well-defined landmarks, pitfalls, and resting places along the way. The idea of the journey can be used to encourage and strengthen those who seek the intangible goals of the spiritual life. Although its value for such purposes cannot be denied, when we use the journey in this way we are short-circuiting the Noah Paradox. Noah's dilemma was that the battle could not be won once, for all time; he knew that every year he would have to confront seedtime and then all the anxiety and struggle until harvest. The idea of the journey, on the other hand, suggests that we pass this way only once, that we must climb the mountain only once. But the Noah Paradox hypothesizes that we climb up, down, and up, again and again.

The traditional spiritual journey comprises five major stages in a linear pattern: awakening, purgation, illumination, dark night of the soul, and union. However, too often we find in our own lives that we awaken only to fall back to sleep, and we must awaken several more times before we are fully awake. Also, illumination is wonderful but momentary: it comes and it goes, and we eagerly await its return. In biographies of the spiritually enlightened, we often read of someone's intense devotion, insights, and seemingly unshakable faith. Yet in other, perhaps more honest biographies and in many autobiographies we note that after a time of intense nearness to God, people can squabble with those closest to them or feel deeply morose about faults they have been unable to correct. Thus, the literal concept of the journey is not usually directly applicable to one's actual spiritual life.

Despite the limitation of its linear character, the symbol of the journey has won an enduring place among the techniques used for self-understanding, because it reflects our realization that the self is a process unfolding over time. At heart, the journey symbolizes transformation rather than static identity. Therefore, it can help us explore the second transformative way, spirituality.

The traditional spiritual way of experiencing the presence of God can be explained using the metaphor of the journey. The journey motif—embracing journeys within or after life, within this world or to another, by a hero or an ordinary believer—is central to most civilizations, mythologies, and religious traditions. The metaphor combines two elements, space and time—it is space unfolding over time. When life is conceived of as a journey, then, time reveals to us different aspects of ourselves, of our relationships, and of our insights into our experiences. We can understand a journey in terms of its destination or in terms of our motivation for journeying. The destination may be a better state of being, such as a journey from slavery to freedom. The journey may also be a return, when we have lost our way: "Mid-way in the journey of our life I came to myself in a dark wood where the straight way was lost."[1]

We are, but we are in process. The journey is one way of expressing this truth. It captures the sense of transformation that is essential to human life.

Six Aspects of the Exodus Journey

Motivations

Motivations for journeys can be either negative (awareness of bondage, consciousness of sin) or positive (love and desire). The Exodus journey is initiated by God and then Moses. The Exodus story offers one version of how we deal with suffering. Sometimes suffering can come so gradually that we aren't even aware of it. That is why the Egyptian taskmasters had to become even more cruel before the Hebrews would follow Moses. We can so constrict our hopes and expectations that we become unconscious of our suffering, yet we are still limited by it. We must somehow break free, but we are too frightened to take responsibility for our actions. Remember, too, that the Hebrews' suffering did not end with their journey out of Egypt. They left captivity without food or shelter, not knowing where they would obtain sustenance. Life is not a single heroic act; instead, it consists of daily calls for repeated acts and for mustering the courage to live. By instilling in the Hebrews the idea of a promised land and thus giving them hope, God allowed them to believe in a world of unlimited possibilities and dreams. By this account of Exodus, then, awareness of our suffering can motivate us to journey as a way of breaking free from suffering.

Obstacles

Every journey has its obstacles. Most obvious are the external obstacles, such as the Egyptians who tried to prevent the Hebrews from leaving and later pursued them. Once we have removed or avoided the external obstacles, we can see the internal obstacles more clearly. For example, the Hebrews in exile yearned for the flesh-pots of Egypt. They feared entering the Promised Land even after repeated experiences of God's support, so they had to remain in the wilderness until the slave generation had died off.

Goals

The immediate goal of the Hebrews' journey out of Egypt was their liberation from slavery. But their testing in the wilderness made them aware of a much greater goal: becoming a holy people. As our goals change during a journey, so does our sense of who will benefit from the journey.

Beneficiary of the Journey

The Hebrews first believed that they themselves would be the sole beneficiaries of their journey: "We were slaves, now we are free."[2] Eventually they came to understand that their own God was *the* God, Creator of Heaven and Earth. That understanding awakened a desire to contribute to all of God's creation, and just how to contribute was formulated in terms of the revelation at Mount Sinai.

Changes in the traveler

At Sinai the Hebrews were transformed from an oppressed, fearful horde into a bold people with a strong sense of mission. We would face repeated periods of oppression over the intervening millenia but would never again be a purposeless horde. Our sense of peoplehood— a shared identity based on the revelation at Mount Sinai—would sustain us in many foreign lands.

Destinations

Over time the Promised Land has continued to beckon, but less and less as a geographical location and more as the spiritual state in which our lives in this world would be filled with holiness. God led the Hebrews' journey through the wilderness by signaling God's presence either within or outside the Tabernacle. When God was within the Tabernacle, the Children of Israel were to pitch camp; when God was outside, they were to break camp and journey. The true goal of the journey lay in the Hebrews' learning to follow God's direction.

The journey may entail some external changes, but it is essentially about internal transformation. We fear change, but we would die without it. We keep trying to hold onto an earlier stage of our life, even when that earlier stage represents the fleshpots of Egypt. As we continue to change, we are constantly pushing forward into the unknown future. Our constantly changing understanding of our present causes us to keep rewriting the past in light of our current insights.

Exodus and the Allegory of the Cave

In some significant respects, the story of the Exodus of the Children of Israel from Egypt resembles Plato's Allegory of the Cave in the *Republic*. In Plato's story, the characters are imprisoned in a subterranean cave. They have been chained, since childhood, by the leg and neck, facing the back wall of the cave. They are unable to turn around and see the sources of the shadows on the wall of the cave. Like Plato's prisoners, the Children of Israel, while they were in Egypt, were unable to recognize that they were in bondage, because they had been slaves for so long that they no longer could conceive of an alternative existence. Plato describes one prisoner who is released and led out of the cave to see the sun for the first time. His eyes are at first blinded by the bright light, but at last he understands that all he had seen in the past had been shadows on a wall. Moved by compassion for his fellow prisoners, he returns to the cave to free the others, only to be mocked by them. They even try to kill him in order to avoid learning the truth.

Raised outside the fetters of slavery but still in the cave of Egypt, Moses is forced to flee Egypt when it is discovered that he slew an Egyptian taskmaster. During his stay in Midian his eyes become accustomed to a new light, so that he is able to see the burning bush. He reluctantly agrees to return to Egypt, although he is fairly certain that his message will not be accepted. His belief in this regard is not unwarranted. The Children of Israel feel he has made them onerous to the Egyptians. Even when they are finally freed from Egypt, they regularly attack Moses, unable to share his vision of the light.

The resemblance between the two texts is important, because the goal in the Allegory of the Cave is not simply to remove the fetters of the prisoners but to transform their vision of reality. This insight may help us realize that the goal in the Exodus story is not simply to remove the conditions of slavery but to transform the vision of reality, and concomitant values, of the Children of Israel.

Exodus can be read as an account of a spiritual journey. It begins with the spiritual state of bondage, albeit to some extent an *unconscious* bondage. It is only when Moses returns with the appeal to let his people go that the Egyptians make the life of the Hebrews bitter with labor, and the unconscious bondage becomes a conscious one. Yet the account of the deliverance from Egypt occupies only the first fifteen chapters of Exodus. Thus, a spiritual journey is not simply a deliverance from a state of bondage. Even the revelation at Mount Sinai does not form the climax of the book. If the end of a spiritual journey is not revelation, what is it? It is day-to-day life in this world. That is why the latter part of Exodus is concerned with minute rules for regulating life in the Promised Land.

Exodus and the Five Stages of the Spiritual Journey

The stages of the Exodus conform to the five stages of the spiritual journey, as mapped out early in this century by Evelyn Underhill: awakening, purgation, illumination, dark night of the soul, and union. *Awakening* refers to our becoming aware that our prior ways of being, thinking, and valuing have been erroneous. In terms of Plato's Allegory of the Cave, awakening would correspond to the prisoners' awareness that they are in chains and would lead to their turning away from the cave wall to face the distant exit. *Purgation* refers to a period of trial, tempering, and discipline that reshapes our values. In the Allegory of the Cave, this stage corresponds to the struggle to leave the cave and the gradual habituation of the prisoners' eyes to sunlight. *Illumination* refers to the new insight that we are now prepared to absorb. In the Allegory of the Cave, this stage corresponds to the actual vision of the sun. *The dark night of the soul* refers to the darkness that follows insight. In the Allegory of the Cave, it corresponds to the blindness caused by going from the sunlight back to the darkened cave. As Plato points out, the eye can be blinded by going either from darkness to light or from light to darkness. *Unity* or *union* refers to that time when our last resistance to change has been removed. We are now entirely united to the values to which we first awakened. For some mystics, union occurs after death and is identified with a beatific vision. Plato does not explicitly delineate the stage of union in his story, but his life, which he spent in spreading his vision, serves as a powerful expression of what union ultimately signifies.

If we wish to interpret the transformation of the Children of Israel as depicted in Exodus in terms of the traditional stages of the spiritual life, we arrive at the following conclusions. Awakening comes about in Egypt after the taskmasters have increased the Hebrews' burden; then, at last, the Children of Israel recognize their status as slaves. Purgation occurs in the wilderness, where the Israelites increasingly learn to trust, through the daily appearance of manna, and come to recognize the source of their blessings. Illumination takes place at Mount Sinai; at this most exalted moment, the people cry out with one voice, "All that the Lord has spoken we will do!" (Exod. 19:8). While Moses is still on the mountain, the Children of Israel experience the dark night of the soul and ask Aaron to make them a golden calf. After the experience of illumination, with its tremendous intimacy with God, there is a fear of God's absence. Trust grows gradually from the initial awakening, but it is still fragile at this point. In building the calf, the Israelites attempt to control what can only be freely given—the sense of presence. The Children of Israel, moving beyond the dark night, help build the Tabernacle in which the Presence will reside. They would still harbor doubts and still fall back in the future, but their essential stance as the people of the covenant has been established; they have reached the goal of their journey—unity with God.

Moses' Journey and the Five Stages

In some significant respects, Moses' biography fore-shadows the Children of Israel's experience. He was rescued from death by royal decree, just as they were. He faced death by water and was rescued by Pharoah's daughter, even as they faced death by water at the Sea of Reeds and were taken across to safety. Moses fled into the desert after his murder of the Egyptian had been discovered, and the Children of Israel went into the wilderness after fleeing Egypt. And Moses' meeting with God on the sacred mountain foreshadows the Children of Israel's meeting at Sinai. Given the similarities between the two stories, it might be helpful to match episodes in Moses' life with the five stages of awakening, purgation, illumination, dark night of the soul, and unity.

Moses' awakening seems to have come when he visited his kinsfolk and witnessed their toil. He awakened to the injustice of their situation. His response, striking down the Egyptian, led to the second stage, purgation. This stage, a time of discipline and of transforming habits and acquiring practices of attentiveness and prayer, occurred in the wilderness. As a shepherd, far from the palace in which he had been raised, he was gradually prepared for the third stage, illumination, which occurred at the burning bush.

You may wonder how, after this overwhelming revelation, there could be a dark night of the soul. Yet, in the next chapter there is the puzzling nocturnal attack on Moses on the road back to Egypt: "At a night encampment on the way, the Lord encountered him and sought to kill him. So Zipporah took a flint and cut off her son's foreskin, and touched his legs with it, saying, 'You are truly a bridegroom of blood to me!' And when He let him alone, she added, 'A bridegroom of blood because of the circumcision'" (Exod. 4:24-26). It seems strange that there should be such terror after the intimacy at the burning bush, and yet terror is part of the whole spiritual process.

> We know from the life of the founders of religion . . . that there is such an 'event of the night'; the sudden collapse of the newly won certainty, the 'deadly factual' moment when the demon working with apparently unbounded authority appears in the world where God had been in control but a moment before. . . . The account of the manner in which God meets Moses as a demon . . . is the unmistakable language of a tradition which also points to the obscure yet perceptible threshold of experience.[3]

This is the experience we have been calling the dark night of the soul.

The realization of unity is described in Exodus 33. Speaking for himself now and not as a representative of the Children of Israel, Moses requests,

> "Oh, let me behold Your Presence!" And He answered, "I will make all My goodness pass before you, and I will proclaim before you the name of the Lord, and the grace that I grant and the compassion that I show. But," He said, "you cannot see My face, for man may not see Me and live." And the Lord said, "See, there is a place near Me. Station yourself on the rock and, as My Presence

passes by, I will put you in a cleft of the rock and shield you with My hand until I have passed by. Then I will take My hand away and you will see My back; but My face must not be seen" (Exod. 33:18–23).

After that experience of deep intimacy with God, Moses still had to deal with a number of problems: the grumblings of the Children of Israel; the problems of water, food, attacks, and rebellions; and, finally, God's denial of his request to enter into the Promised Land.

The Journey of the Egyptians

We've been looking at the book of Exodus as an account of a journey, or, more precisely as the account of *two* journeys: Moses' and the Children of Israel's. But there is also the journey made by the Egyptians. Their journey begins with Pharoah's question "Who is God?" and ends with an awareness of the answer to the question. The awareness is achieved first by the magicians, then by the Egyptian people, and later, if at all, by Pharoah. Awareness is reached through the ten plagues.

In a way, the plagues imitate the Creation account in Genesis. God's presence causes creation, or construction, and the gradual withdrawal of that presence causes de-construction. The first plague is the transformation of water into blood. This is paralleled in Genesis by God's spirit hovering over the waters. During the fourth plague, the swarms of insects, a division is made between the Children of Israel and the Egyptians. We noted earlier that division is an important creative principle. The division made at this point creates a people. The plague of livestock disease reminds us that the well-being of animals comes from God. And the infliction of boils shows us that the well-being of people comes

from God as well. The plague of hail attacks the fruitfulness of the earth, as do the locusts. Further, the
locusts attack not only the current fruitfulness but the
future fruitfulness as well.

Darkness, the next-to-last plague, powerfully brings
us back to the creation of light at the onset of creation.
But there is an important difference between the two
darknesses. Whereas the darkness in Genesis is pregnant
with life, the plague of darkness is a prelude to death.
The death of the firstborn makes clear that God is the
source of life and distance from God is death. To work
our way through an analysis of the plagues, to understand their formulation as an answer to the question,
"Who is God?" is to go on a journey. Pharoah was not
open to this journey. But we can assume that there were
reflective, sensitive Egyptians at the time who were
aware of Moses' warnings to Pharoah and who witnessed
the plagues. They might have simply become terrified
or bitter. But they might also have obtained insights
similar to those described above.

We have discussed spirituality, the second of the transformative ways, in terms of the journey. Creativity can
also be seen as a journey. In the transformative way of
creativity, we create the world and let the creative process
transform us and our relationship to the world. In the
transformative way of spirituality, we focus directly on
creating ourselves. But the difference between creating
the world and creating ourselves is not as great as one
might imagine. We tend to use one phrase or the other
in order to indicate the type of object we are creating.
In creativity, we focus explicitly on the external world;
in spirituality, we focus on our internal being. But we
are no less creative when we focus on our internal being:
" . . . art creates r.ature, including human nature."[4] In
this crucial respect the spiritual journey *is* the journey
of creativity. Therefore, the steps in Genesis that we
have already outlined remain a key to the spiritual way.

We can expect the stages of the spiritual way to exhibit the characteristics we have already found in the stages of the creative way.

Chaos and void is a necessary stage not only in creativity but also in spirituality. On the spiritual journey there are repeated examples of the breaking down of categories and the opening up of fresh relationships via changes in roles, shaking up of assumptions, and so on. We see this in Moses' life, during which he changes from prince in the palace of Pharoah, to fugitive in Midian, to leader of a horde of slaves. We see it in the life of the Children of Israel, who change from an enslaved people to a holy people. Both the creative and the spiritual way rely on trust, for the first step is darkness, the darkness of not knowing our way and of loss and chaos. But in the process of trusting, something begins to grow. Along with the trust and the incipient fruitfulness comes the imperative to let go. A deeper transformation is at stake. Just as the darkness before creation is essentially fruitful, so is the darkness and uncertainty of the spiritual way. The correct response is to trust, cease resisting, and be transformed. Just as creativity involves moments of fear, so does the spiritual way. We fear we will be changed beyond what we can imagine ourselves to be. But if we are to face the Noah Paradox, the ongoingness of time in the face of devastation, the world has to be shattered and then re-formed. There is loss, but it is followed by breakthroughs. As the Sufi aphorism puts it, "When the heart weeps for what it has lost, the spirit laughs for what it has found."[5]

6. The Way of Love: The Song of Songs

We have explored two transformative ways: creativity, which focuses on an external creation even while it changes the creator, and spirituality, which focuses on internal change while it alters our relationship with the world. The third transformative way, the one most readily available to us, is the way of love. Like all transformative ways, the way of love entails breaking up our inherited sense of self, followed by confusion, a growing trust, and a renewed vision of the world. In creativity, transformation is associated with an external product. In spirituality, transformation aims explicitly at a new sense of self. In the way of love, our goal is again transformation, both in the external world and in our internal notion of self—a transformation that gives us the capacity for disinterested love.

One way to consider the transformative way of love is through our role as parents. Becoming parents initiates a special journey of love. We learn to love the life the mother carries within her before it is born. We love the infant that cannot even focus its eyes on us. We love and we give, and we feel remarkable tenderness as we observe the tremulous growth of the child. Eventually, however, the deep, empathetic love we feel for the infant becomes inappropriate and restrictive when the child runs off after playmates. Soon, we discover what it is to love an adolescent who rejects us. (Is this what is meant by loving your enemies?) We care ardently but have learned to temper the expression of this care.

Finally, the infant, child, adolescent, becomes an adult. We still care, but now we must love this offspring as an independent being. We are drawn, sometimes willingly, frequently resistingly and painfully, into disinterested love. We brought a life into this world and this life continues—sometimes, it seems, without even a backward glance at us. At this time we might reflect on the course of our love for God. God has dealt with our infancy, childhood, adolescent rebellion, and egocentric early adulthood. What do we feel first? Gratitude? Embarrassment at the picture of ourselves revealed by this line of thought? Or tenderness for God's and our shared pain?

While the way of love is the most readily available transformative way, access to it is complicated because *love* is such a vague word, almost an excuse for loose thinking. *Love* can refer to an emotion, a mode of action, or a way of thinking. Traditionally, the way of love has been set up in opposition to the way of knowledge. Knowledge, as the West defines it, gives power. You can control ideas. The Western view of love usually involves a loss of control, a weakness. But the biblical view of knowledge is not distinct from love. Biblical knowledge confers vulnerability; it opens the knower to new experiences and is therefore transformative. The knower, who is the lover, must be willing to be vulnerable and to change. This type of knowledge gives, not power, but a type of weakness that engenders life: tenderness. The love that enables us to face and overcome the Noah Paradox must be a love that opens us to change.

"All evils seem to have arisen from the fact that happiness or unhappiness is made wholly to depend on the quality of the object which we love. When a thing is not loved, no quarrels will arise concerning it—no sadness will be felt if it perishes—no envy if it is possessed by another—no fear, no hatred, in short no disturbances of the mind."[1] Spinoza's objective in this quotation is not to keep us from loving, but rather to make us aware of how central our loving is to all other emotions and how the improper understanding of the object of our love leads us to unrealistic expectations and so to suffering. The solution he offers in *On the Improvement of the Understanding* is not immediately accessible to most readers. He offers, in lieu of our perishable objects of love, "love toward a thing eternal and infinite [which] feeds the mind wholly with joy and is itself unmingled with any sadness, wherefore it is greatly to be desired and sought for with all our strength." The way to this love is spelled out in the first four books of his *Ethics*. It culminates in his statement, "The intellectual love of the mind toward God is that very love with which He loves Himself . . . that is to say, the intellectual love of the mind toward God is part of the infinite love with which God loves Himself."[2]

The problem is that we don't know what to love or, perhaps, how to love. We keep focusing on the wrong thing or in the wrong way, so that, regardless of our best intentions and efforts, love is behind our deepest pain and suffering. It is hard to believe and even harder to accept that, even in the face of death, one is still fighting jealousy, mourning thwarted dreams, testing the bounteous supporting love. To test, to ask for proof, to close one's hand over the freely proffered gift: to clutch. The necessary motion is as simple, as natural, as effortless, as the exhaling of air. Let go. Trust and let go. Be open and let go. And that letting go, that release, is freedom and love. Oh joy!

The Love of the Mind for God

Spinoza offers a radical correction to our usual way of thinking about love. He is correcting both the object of and the way of love. In Spinoza's view, the proper object of love is God. That does not entail a turning away from this world or a rejection of the love between two people. Rather it requires us to perceive our beloved deeply enough to penetrate to where we can find God's presence in our beloved. So we may indeed love our beloved with "his head [of] finest gold, his locks... curled and black as a raven" (Song of Songs 5:11). But if we love him *because* of his curly black hair we will be dismayed when he grows bald. His curly black hair may serve an analogous function to that of the burning bush. The hair causes us "to turn aside to look at this marvelous sight," but what we should seek is the holy *signaled* by the sight. Spinoza also suggests that the gift is not to *be* loved but to be capable of loving. Our capacity to love *is* God's love for us. We learn to love by being loved. We have all been loved or we would not be alive. Love is essential for our being and well-being. When we discover our immense capacities for love, caring, and tenderness, we are surprised. We did not know that we could be so generous, so unselfish. We tend to think that these marvelous gifts are occasioned by the object of our love. But Spinoza suggests that they are the gift of our having been loved.

When we were younger we sometimes thought it would be wonderful if we were loved by everyone. The *receiving* of love appeared to be the most desirable gift. But as we grew in experience and insight, we recognized that it was *our* loving that enriched our world. The more we loved, the more we looked forward to meeting people, hearing music we had taken time to get to know, seeing plants that we cared about, the more dear our world became. All we loved made life more lovable. The people who loved us whom we did not love were *not* a gift; frequently they were a burden. So the gift was not to *be* loved, but to love. There were few problems associated with the art, the music, the plants, or even the pets we loved. The problems usually arose when the

God. If Akiba was right, then we must reread this biblical text in the hope of discerning a way to overcome the Noah Paradox.

Oh, give me of the kisses of your mouth.

This first line makes it clear that love is experiential. We seek the experience of the beloved. Certainly, in the beginning, we discover love through our feelings. However, true love is not feeling, any more than the burning bush *is* God. Instead, the burning bush signals the presence of God, and intense emotions signal the presence of love.

But what is it we love? In the beginning, the lover is the person you desire to have kiss you with the kisses of his or her mouth. Gradually, we recognize that contained in the love of our beloved is a love that is more constant, more enduring, and all-consuming. The experience gained as we grow older allows us to strip away the attachments and false loves that have distracted us. This pruning allows us to see our previous loves, both in their falsity and in their deepest truth. Love of wealth, status, and sensual pleasures are challenged naturally as part of the maturation process; we discover their inadequacies over time. But there is also something true in such false loves. The Song of Songs leads us to a recognition of the underlying truth in *all* our loves.

Oh, give me of the kisses of your mouth.

This is such a grand opening. And yet we hesitate. *Do* we, *can* we unambiguously assert that? We hesitate. Our experience may have revealed a recurrent pattern in which feelings of bliss, joy, and peace have come during times of meditation, hard work, and reflection. They have *not* come from wealth, status, sensual pleasures. Anything less than love opening out to the divine has finally turned sour in our mouth. But that has not stopped the craving for such false loves.

He rained meat on them like dust

winged birds like the sands of the sea,
making them come down inside His camp,
around His dwelling-place.
They ate till they were sated;
He gave them what they craved.
They had not yet wearied of what they craved;
the food was still in their mouths
when God's anger flared up at them.
(Ps. 78:27–31)

What we crave is still in our mouths when anger flares up or, in other words, the object of our love has led to our suffering or destruction. We do not know the right thing to love.

For your love is more delightful than wine.

Wine changes our vision of reality, as does love. Love is the ultimate intoxication, delivering, not a delirium, but the deepest reality. I started keeping a diary when my daughter was born, and as I fell ever more deeply in love with her, I saw the world with increasing clarity and appreciation. Everything I experienced was something I could share with her. I experienced the autumn air as I had not experienced it since early childhood. I noticed squirrels and pigeons that I had long before ceased to see. Even the motes of dust swirling in a light beam became something I could enjoy and share with her. Love did not blind me. I became more aware of potential dangers: sharp corners, unexpected steps, open electrical sockets. Love is more delightful than wine and more potent.

Your ointments yield a sweet fragrance

The sense of smell is the earliest, most primitive sense. A specific odor can take us back to earliest childhood. For example, the smell of pipe tobacco, of leaves burning, or of something cooking as we pass a window can arouse longings for the past we cannot define.

Your name is like finest oil

When we are first in love we usually find every possible reason to speak of our beloved. We want to say our loved one's name in order to hear it. To speak our beloved's name is an experience that is thrilling, embarrassing, and filled with memories and intimate associations. If we repeated the name all day long, would it finally become ordinary? No! For the name changes everything around it. When we think of the name, we think of moments of intimacy, fear, awe, and joy. All of this becomes associated with the name. Now, at last, we can understand what the mystics were doing when they combined the letters of God's name and chanted. However many times we say or think the name, associations and thoughts keep flooding in.

Draw me after you, let us run!

Running is the motion inherent in the way of love. We do not, at this point, seek rest or peace, but motion. We are so far away from the beloved that we need all the speed we can muster: Let us run!

I am dark but comely,
O daughters of Jerusalem

When we are in love, there comes a moment when we wonder what our beloved sees when he or she sees us. Were it not for our beloved's love we could not bear this reflection, this introspection. But the love in his eyes allows us to affirm that "I am comely," even as we recognize that "I am dark."

Don't stare at me because I am swarthy,
Because the sun has gazed upon me.

If our beloved's patient, loving smile has allowed us to change from dark to comely, then focusing on our own or another's darkness is not the right way. Loving acceptance is the way, not harsh judgment.

I am a rose of Sharon,
A lily of the valleys.
Like a lily among thorns,
So is my darling among the maidens.

We are asked to look at our own beauty and giftedness. But to look at them is really to look at love's gift to us. We are lovable because we have been loved.

> *I adjure you, O maidens of Jerusalem,*
> *By gazelles or by hinds of the field:*
> *Do not wake or rouse*
> *Love until it please!*

Love cannot be forced, rushed or programmed; it is a gift. All we can do is be open, receptive, aware, and attentive. Because love is a gift, we grow impatient waiting for it. We keep wanting to control love. Our impatience and lack of trust reflect our insecurity about whether or when our beloved will come. These are the same feelings we have about our relationship with God. The time has come to trust—God's love, care, ways, and timetable.

> *My beloved spoke thus to me,*
> *"Arise, my darling;*
> *My fair one, come away!"*

Such a moving call; how can we resist! Why *should* we resist? The call is irresistible.

> *For now the winter is past,*
> *The rains are over and gone.*

All the pain, the coldness, the deadness is gone. All the tears and sorrow are past.

> *The blossoms have appeared in the land,*
> *The time of singing has come;*

All is a song of love. Spring is a glorious Hallelujah.

> *The song of the turtledove*
> *Is heard in our land.*

It is a haunting, melancholy, and nostalgic song, a yearning.

> *The green figs form on the figtree,*
> *The vines in blossom give off fragrance.*

These are images of such intense beauty, life, passion. All life is celebrating.

> *Arise, my darling;*

My fair one, come away!
O my dove, in the cranny of the rocks,
Hidden by the cliff,
Let me see your face.

Suddenly we are back with Moses and his desire to
see God face to face, and God's consent to hide him
in the cleft of the rock. Moses, speaking for himself and
not as a representative of the Children of Israel, pleads
with God, "'Oh, let me behold Your Presence!' And
He answered, 'I will make all My goodness pass before
you, . . . But, you cannot see My face, for man may not
see Me and live. See, there is a place near Me. Station
yourself on the rock and, as My Presence passes by, I
will put you in a cleft of the rock and shield you with
My hand until I have passed by'" (Exod. 33:18–23).
Could Moses really love God the way the lover loves
the beloved in the Song of Songs? "Love toward a thing
eternal and infinite feeds the mind wholly with joy and
is itself unmingled with any sadness, wherefore it is
greatly to be desired and sought for with all our
strength."[3] That is precisely what Spinoza has suggested
we do. His suggestion is *not* restrictive. The love of God
is the most expansive of all types of love. So the suggestion that we love God also recommends that we be
open to all types of love. Particularly, it does not rule
out our intense love for our beloved. Rather, it makes
us realize that, when we truly love our beloved, we are
loving God.

Catch us the foxes,
The little foxes
That ruin the vineyards.

The expression "little foxes" is deceptive. As soon as
we see the word *little* we tend to think that the foxes,
whatever they may symbolize, are not serious or dangerous. That is a potential trap. Foxes can grow large
enough to destroy our fruitfulness. This line refers to
the fact that it is not enough to know *what* to love, we

have to learn *how* to love. *How* to love entails catching
the foxes, which are the petty annoyances, peeves, griev-
ances, and small-minded patterns of thought that destroy love.

> *Upon my couch at night*
> *I sought the one I love—*
> *I sought, but found him not.*

You cannot find your love by wishing or dreaming.
It is true that love often begins by changing the shape
of our dreams, but that is only a first step.

> *I must rise and roam the town*
> *Through the streets and through the squares;*
> *I must seek the one I love.*

Active seeking is required, not just a transformed
desire, but a transformed life.

> *I sought but found him not.*
> *I met the watchmen*
> *Who patrol the town.*
> *"Have you seen the one I love?"*
> *Scarcely had I passed them*
> *When I found the one I love.*

We must seek actively and be willing to publicly state
what we seek. Those we tell will not find our beloved
for us, but our indifference to their opinion and total
focus on our search are required for success in love.

> *I held him fast, I would not let him go*
> *Till I brought him to my mother's house,*
> *To the chamber of her who conceived me.*

The one I find, grasp, and hold fast must be made
personal and intimate by being brought to my mother's
house. In other words: I found in the core of my being
the love that I first thought was outside me and elusive.
Now I find him in my house.

> *I adjure you, O maidens of Jerusalem,*
> *By gazelles or by hinds of the fields:*
> *Do not wake or rouse*
> *Love until it please!*

When we read of the beloved's union, of being held fast, not letting go until we bring him to our mother's chambers, we are tempted, to follow suit even though we have not yet been called. To give in to the temptation is dangerous. We must wait for love to call us.

Ah, you are fair, my darling,
Ah, you are fair.
Your eyes are like doves
Behind your veil.
Your hair is like a flock of goats
Streaming down Mount Gilead.
Your teeth are like a flock of ewes
Climbing up from the washing pool;
All of them bear twins,
And not one loses her young.
Your lips are like a crimson thread,
Your mouth is lovely.

This is a powerful description of the beloved's physical beauty. But the imagery is that of a child. Our first sense of ourself comes when we are reflected in our mother's eyes. We look into her eyes, pull her hair, put our fingers in her mouth. When our mother looks at us and sees *us* and not some sense of herself through her relationship with us—that is, when she mirrors us perfectly—we feel whole and lovable. But none of us has been *perfectly* mirrored by our mother. However, just as the Children of Israel were given a second set of Tablets of the Law, we are all given a second chance. Through love we are given another chance to be looked upon and perfectly mirrored.

Then comes a section as puzzling and confusing as the building of the golden calf in Exodus.

I was asleep,
But my heart was wakeful.
Hark, my beloved knocks!
"Let me in, my own,
My darling, my faultless dove!

For my head is drenched with dew,
My locks with the damp of night."

Instead of responding to his call she rationalizes.

I had taken off my robe—
Was I to don it again?
I had bathed my feet—
Was I to soil them again?

She hesitates, a hesitation so unlike her earlier acceptance and eagerness.

My beloved took his hand off the latch,
And my heart was stirred for him.
I rose to let in my beloved;
My hands dripped myrrh—
My fingers, flowing myrrh—
Upon the handles of the bolt. . . .
But my beloved had turned and gone.

Often, we do not think enough of what is at stake in a relationship. In the beginning, as in parenting, it is often one-sided. The lover gives and gives and loves and loves. But when we finally recognize and embrace the lover, to turn away momentarily may cause him or her to turn away as well. Until we truly know our beloved, we cannot speak of our beloved's turning away. But when we know the beloved and the relationship has deepened, to turn away is an act of unfaithfulness.

I was faint because of what he said.
I sought, but found him not;
I called, but he did not answer.

This sounds far too familiar. The carelessness we have sometimes felt after first awakening to love leads far too often to loss of the beloved and the destruction of the relationship.

I met the watchmen
Who patrol the town;
They struck me, they bruised me.
The guards of the walls
Stripped me of my mantle.

Suddenly, without the love that had transformed our world, we are vulnerable. External forces hurt us in ways they could not before.

Whither has your beloved gone,
O fairest of women? . . .
My beloved has gone down to his garden,
To the beds of spices,
To browse in the gardens
And to pick lilies.

Although we do not always respond as we ought, we *do* know our beloved. We know where he can be found and what he will be doing. A deep confidence pervades our spirit.

In the text, the compliments are repeated, but the repetition reinforces their meaning rather than boring the listener.

I went down to the nut grove . . .
To see if the vines had blossomed,
If the pomegranates were in bloom.

Up to now, we have generally been concerned with the literal meaning of the text. But there is a traditional interpretation of this passage that holds that the nut garden is a symbol of true interiority. Hence, to go down to the nut grove is to check the condition of one's soul to see whether it is fruitful and mature. In a symbolic interpretation of this section of the book, we see an initial call, a moment of hesitancy and even unfaithfulness, then a need to check the condition of the soul. Has it really awakened to the call of love?

Come my beloved,
Let us go into the open;
Let us lodge among the henna shrubs.
Let us go early to the vineyards;
Let us see if the vine has flowered,
If its blossoms have opened,
If the pomegranates are in bloom.
There I will give my love to you.

We will be together in all places now, even in the
open. Away from the closed intimacy of interiority, we
will now be ever together in the openness of the villages
and fields. Together we will inspect all that has grown
up around us, through us, because of us.

> *Who is she that comes up from the desert,*
> *Leaning upon her beloved?*

The desert is a place of stripping away, of trial and
emptiness. It is devoid of landmarks, filled with fear and
confusion. But here the desert image has been transformed in a critically important fashion. Formerly a
place of solitude and isolation, the desert now contains
the lover and the beloved, on whose arm the lover leans.
As Hosea said: "Assured, I will speak coaxingly to her
and lead her through the wilderness and speak to her
tenderly. . . . There she shall respond as in the days of
her youth when she came up from the land of Egypt"
(Hosea 2:16). The images of trial and purgation traditionally associated with the desert are here transformed
into an image of intimacy.

> *Let me be a seal upon your heart,*
> *Like the seal upon your hand.*
> *For love is fierce as death.*

We love, even though we know that what we love
must die. We continue to love even after what we love
has died. In love we recover what we have loved and
lost. Our love opens out to that which cannot be lost.

As we read the text and follow the emotions, questions
remain: Whom are we to love, and how ought we to
love? It is one thing for Moses to love God, but our
love seems much more earthly. The text speaks clearly
of a physical person with curly hair. It is true that we
should love God. It is also true that we should love
physical persons. There is no contradiction between
these statements. Far too often, "we avoid transcendence
through immanence and go straight to transcendence,
producing bloodless words with no grounding."[4] But the

way to transcendence *is* through immanence. In other words, the way to the love of God is through the love of this world and its creatures. There *is* no love of God that is separate from a love of the physical things in this world. But, "all evils seem to have arisen from the fact that happiness or unhappiness is made wholly to depend on the quality of the object which we love." Aren't we supposed to seek "love toward a thing eternal and infinite [which] feeds the mind wholly with joy"?[5] In order to do so, we must love finite, imperfect, particular people, and we are to love them in a way that opens out to transcendent, eternal, infinite God.

The Song of Songs and Diotima's Speech

Earlier, we used Plato's "Allegory of the Cave" to help us better understand Exodus. Following a similar approach, we will use Diotima's speech from Plato's *Symposium* to shed further light on the Song of Songs. Diotima's speech is divided into two parts. The first is a general discussion about the relationship of love and death, and our desire for the "deathless." The second focuses on the path of initiation, analogous to the way of the spiritual journey.

Diotima begins her speech by saying that a mortal creature "cannot, like the divine, be still the same throughout eternity; it can only leave behind new life to fill the vacancy that is left in its species by obsolescence. This, my dear Socrates, is how the body and all else that is temporal partakes of the eternal; there is no other way."[6] Diotima offers no way for us to participate in immortality other than by leaving a biological or spiritual offspring or a "deathless" name behind. But while her statement *explicitly* rules out other forms of immortality for mortals, it *implicitly* suggests another answer. The world of eternal, unchanging forms is

related to our changing, temporal world of becoming
through *methexus*, that is, participation. Our world of
becoming doesn't *imitate* the eternal world of being, it
participates in it. That is, there is an unchanging, eternal
aspect to being that is discoverable in and through
becoming. In other words, transcendence is approached
through immanence. This point is powerfully illustrated
in the second part of Diotima's speech, which concentrates on the path of initiation.

The candidate for initiation to wisdom should "fall
in love with the beauty of one individual body." Here
is the burning bush, the curly, raven-black hair, which
is the sign of the holy. "Next he must consider how
nearly the beauty of one body is like the beauty of
another." In other words, love, as Spinoza defined it,
leads to self-expansion. The world is enlarged for the
lover. "Next he must grasp that the beauties of the body
are as nothing to the beauties of the soul." Here the
candidate must go beyond appearances to reality.

> And from this he will be led to contemplate the beauty
> of laws and institutions. . . . And next his attention should
> be diverted from institutions to the sciences so that he
> may know the beauty of every kind of knowledge. . . . And
> turning his eyes toward the open sea of beauty, he will
> find in such contemplation the seed of the most fruitful
> discourse and the loftiest thought, and reap a golden
> harvest of philosophy, until, confirmed and strengthened,
> he will come upon one single form of knowledge, the
> knowledge of the beauty I am about to speak of. . . . And
> whoever has been initiated so far in the mysteries of Love
> and has viewed all these aspects of the beautiful in due
> succession, is at last drawing near the final revelation.
> And now, Socrates, there bursts upon him that wondrous
> vision which is the very soul of the beauty he has toiled
> so long for. It is an everlasting loveliness which neither
> comes nor goes, which neither flowers nor fades, for such

beauty is the same on every hand, the same then as now, here as there, this way as that way, the same to every worshipper as it is to every other.[7]

Diotima's speech reconfirms our earlier conclusion: our love for the individual opens us up to the beauties of the world, and gradually, to the source of all beauty, God. In the seventh stanza of the Song of Songs, in one of the verses of compliments, the lover says,

Your rounded thighs are like jewels,
The work of a master's hand.

Beauty points beyond itself to its source, just as the burning bush points beyond itself to that which allows it to burn but not be consumed. The expansive nature and ultimate goal of love do not eliminate love for the individual beloved, which begins the path of initiation, but they do keep us from slavish devotion to an individual. We learn to love in a nonpossessive way as our love keeps expanding and becoming more inclusive.

Love and Suffering

Rabbi Akiba, who recommended that we focus on the Song of Songs, also taught the separation between suffering and retribution. The importance of this teaching becomes clear when we consider the following quotation from the Rabbi's writings. "Only he who held that 'suffering is precious' and did not interpret it as an act of justice, for in his opinion 'compassion does not enter into judgment,' could bless for calamity and affliction and designate God in his benediction as 'All-Merciful,' since the suffering did not come as a consequence of justice but as a token of the Lord's love."[8]

Even if we accept this point intellectually, the pain is still there. The reality of love does not negate the reality of pain. It doesn't make the pain disappear, but it does change the perspective of the sufferer. The Song of Songs is a beautiful text on love, but it does not delineate the many types of pain inherent in love. Instead, its focus is on the growing love. But sorrow has caught our attention. In order to explore this issue, we need to read the Song of Songs in conjunction with another biblical text, Lamentations.

Lamentations: we shall learn a new song. "How doth the city sit solitary that was full of people! How is she become as a widow! She that was great among the nations" (Lam. 1:1). In times of mourning, we often turn to Job or Lamentations. Does reading these books increase our sorrow or does it give us perspective on our suffering in the light of greater suffering? Does it offer some insight and comfort?

"How doth the city sit solitary that was full of people!" The first thing we learn from these texts is solitude. How truly alone we are when real sorrow comes. Along with the sorrow and the solitude comes shame. We are no longer beloved of God. How can this have happened to us? Jerusalem loses, one by one, the signs of election, of the chosen state: The heathen are entered into her sanctuary. Appointed seasons and sabbath are caused to be forgotten. King and priest rejected, God's altar is cast off, God's sanctuary is abhorred. The walls of the city are destroyed, the gates are sunk into the ground, instruction is no more. "No vision from the Lord" (Lam. 2:9).

The final destruction of Jerusalem is not the tearing down of the citadels, the profaning of the sanctuaries, the abolition of the festivals, or the rejection of king and priest. The final destruction is the silence of God. No vision from the Lord. No vision. We know from experience what that means. We know the sense of deadness we feel when there can be no more sign. We do not wait for the telephone to ring. We do not eagerly check the mail. We do not notice the signs of changing seasons. These augur nothing. Nothing augurs anything. We feel that there will never again be a vision from the Lord. "How doth the city sit solitary that was full of people!" The destruction of Jerusalem is the loss of the chosen state, of election, of meaning, and of a name. Our name is part of the city, the culture that we live and work in. When our city is destroyed, who are we? "How doth the city sit solitary." Our name is spouse; our name is parent; our name is beloved. We chose the Song of Songs, but we were given Lamentations. "The joy of our heart is ceased. Our dance is turned into mourning." But that is not the end. Jerusalem is destroyed but the people remain. One by one, the signs of being beloved are destroyed, but love remains. In a strange land, they sing your song. In every land, they sing your song. If the citadels are torn down, we shall enshrine them in our heart. If the altars are profaned, our lives shall become an altar. "Turn thou us unto thee, O Lord, and we shall be turned. Renew our days as of old" (Lam. 5:21).

The survivors of Jerusalem were lovers. They turned the vulnerable city of their homeland into an invulnerable ideal within their hearts. Invulnerable! Throughout the intervening centuries, Jerusalem stands, safe, incorruptible, ever-shining. The lovers of Jerusalem turned the worst catastrophe into ultimate triumph. Only now is their true faith revealed, a faith that exists outside the walls and gates of the city. Neither stone nor altar constitutes this Jerusalem; it is the vision of the Lord. We should apprentice ourselves at the feet of the survivors of Jerusalem. We, too, should learn how to transmute defeat into victory. "Turn thou us unto thee, O Lord, and we shall be turned."

The interrelationship of love and pain, the tension between the Song of Songs and Lamentations, brings us back to the heart of the Noah Paradox. Love does not rule out infidelities, faithlessness, hard words, or

angry silences. We are still competitive, defensive, in-
secure, and jealous. Handling our second major argu-
ment with a loved one is nowhere near as difficult as
dealing with the first. We forget that and feel almost
back at square one with the third fight. However, with
each disagreement, there is real progress. We must face
each problem anew, but we have a history of successes
and growing faith. Resolving, not winning fights is what
we want. Yet even if this fight were resolved tomorrow
we would be involved in a new dispute the day after.
What we truly want is to be fully alive, fully growing
and contributing, fully conscious and caring. "Though
much suffering may, indeed will remain, apprehension,
confusion, instability, despair, will cease."[9]

The illness of a loved one challenges our sense of a
loving God. All our vast cosmological speculation is
reduced to the question, Will she recover? With that
reduction comes the realization that there is no secret,
seventh heaven that is more blissful than seeing the
pain medication finally taking effect and easing a loved
one's pain. This world is as wondrous as anything we
will ever see.

Our beloved's illness has left us shaken. Yet sorrow
within the context of love (trust) need not be destructive.
Without the framework of love, sorrow *is* destructive.
Along with all that is negative in the illness, there can
still be great joy and gratitude. We do love God. We
love God in and through our love of our ill loved one,
our family and friends, the cat, the birds, the early
morning silence. We have been given great gifts.

Love causes all the pain we discussed, yet a deeper
absorption in love provides the cure. Love is fiercer than
death and defuses the pain of loss and separation.
Armed with the unshakable knowledge that we are
loved, we can confront all the pains of love. We are
centered on the awareness of our being loved, which
persists when all else is threatened or destroyed.

Pain is real but not final. Destruction is a severe pruning, furthering greater growth. All our struggles in love are taken up in God's love, which never gives up.

The ongoingness of time *means* the ongoingness of time. The search for some magic solution to our problems, some end to the tasks we must face, the anger we must mollify, the impatience we must calm, the fears we must overcome or at least accept: that search has distracted us from what is most real and most urgent. Here and now we are alive. This is reality! This world, as we find it, is our only world. However far we journey, we must return to this place. And so our basic motion is less that of a journey and more one of staying put and beginning to grow more connected to this world.

7. Exodus in the Light of the Song of Songs

We began our exploration by examining the Noah Paradox, the awareness that God's guarantee of the ongoingness of time is, at best, an ambiguous blessing. For those who have suffered, and that includes all of us, the ongoingness of time means the ongoingness of suffering. We then considered the journey model, based on linear progression, which short-circuits the Noah Paradox by picturing life as a limited, one-way adventure with a beginning and an end. But the journey metaphor did not reflect our experience of repeated setbacks. However, there is another metaphor that *can* help us learn to accept the ongoingness of time as gift: a loving relationship.

We are formed in part by the stories with which we are raised. The tales we hear and read in childhood shape the way we understand the world. For example, a consciousness shaped by Grimm's fairy tales differs from one shaped by Dr. Seuss stories. The foundational story in the Jewish tradition is that of the Exodus from Egypt. But the Exodus story can be told in a number of significantly different ways. For each way the Exodus story is told there is a different model of transformation.

The Exodus story essentially consists of six elements: laboring in servitude, being called forth, receiving the Law, wandering in the wilderness, falling back (repeatedly), and entering the Promised Land. We will see that these elements can have very different meanings, depending on the model we choose as a metaphor for the Exodus story.

It took a great rabbinical revolutionary to realize that before the Jews could really change, their formative story would have to be changed. Rabbi Akiba declared that all of Scripture was holy and that the Song of Songs was the holiest book. Akiba read Exodus in terms of the Song of Songs, directly opposing the view of Rabbi Pappos, who interpreted the Song of Songs in terms of Exodus. For example, a line in the Song of Songs compares the beloved to a steed in Pharoah's chariot (1:9). Because, in the normative view, Exodus is the foundational story in the Bible, Pappos naturally interpreted that passage in terms of the Exodus and subsequent verses in terms of the revelation at Sinai. But Akiba offered a startling new vision—of our self-understanding, of our life with God, and of our life with others—that took the Song of Songs as its foundational text. Akiba held that, "if the Torah had not been given to us, the Song of Songs would have sufficed to guide the world."[1] If we take Rabbi Akiba's statement seriously as a starting point for reevaluating our concept of self, God, and other, we trade the Exodus elements of servitude, being called forth, wandering in the wilderness, falling back at the building of the golden calf, and Promised Land for awakening to love, choosing, growing, and commitment, respectively.

If Rabbi Akiba was right, we must return to the Exodus story with a consciousness shaped by the Song of Songs. When we first examined the Exodus story, we did so by using the metaphor of the journey. One of the main reasons we had for accepting the journey model was because it so clearly portrays the motion inherent to life. Life entails motion. Aristotle's discussion of motion (in the *Physics*) distinguishes the different types of motion with unusual clarity. He delineates six types of motion: increase and decrease, changes in quantity; becoming other, a change in quality; coming to be and passing away, changes in substance; and locomotion, or change of place. The journey model uses the category of place to stand for all the other transformations that occur along the way of spiritual growth.

There are some problems with using this model. It suggests, that our path is unidirectional; we pass this way only once. It also suggests that it is *we* who journey even though experience points to a sense of being called. We do not go out alone on a solitary journey. We are called forth and met along the way by that which summoned us. The journey model further suggests that there is a destination to life. But we have learned that we have no final destination in this world. The changes in us are to help us live in this reality. But the essential insight of the journey model remains: life means motion. There must be some way of characterizing this movement. Aristotle's two preferred images of motion are the construction of an artifact, usually a building, and the unfolding of an inherent nature, such as an acorn becoming an oak tree. Those examples also contain the six forms of motion he names. However, as rich as they are in possibilities, the essential question remains: how to deal with the Noah Paradox.

Moses' Deepening Love of God

We can interpret Exodus as the story of a deepening love between God and Moses. We tend not to read it that way, because we usually concern ourselves more with the Children of Israel than with Moses. Yet what happened to Moses happened eventually to the Children of Israel as well: God loved them, chose them, courted them, forgave them, and made a covenant with them.

We all believe that we have been imperfectly loved at one time or another. This belief constitutes a wound or flaw in us. Being called by God would grant us uncon-

ditional love and thus heal our wounds. We know the
story of Moses: hidden in the bulrushes, rescued by
Pharoah's daughter, nursed by his own mother, then
raised by Pharoah's daughter. We know the story, but
only from our point of view. How must it have seemed
to Moses himself? Though raised in Pharoah's palace,
Moses was related by blood to the Egyptian's slaves,
people despised by his foster mother. We obtain some
notion of his true feelings from the incident in which
he killed an Egyptian who had been beating a Hebrew.
He felt tremendous shame that his rage could have
caused him to commit such a rash deed. He fled to
Midian, where he was regarded as an Egyptian by the
daughters of Jethro. Since he did not, apparently, dispute
this assumption, his self-identity must still have been
in question. Standing before the burning bush, his first
reaction was one of curiosity and wonder. Only when
God said, "I am the God of your father, the God of
Abraham, Isaac, and Jacob," did Moses hide his face.
God had singled him out and loved him for the very
identity that he had found problematic. In this episode,
the healing by God's unconditional love of Moses' wound
began. He could not believe that he was loved despite
his wound, so he tested God, using a series of objections:
the Children of Israel wouldn't accept him; they would
want to know God's name; he was slow of speech. But
God continued to reassure Moses by answering his
objections.

There is a curious section in the Song of Songs, in
which the lover comes to his beloved at night, but she
finds reason not to open the door to him (5:2–8). Only
after he has left does she rouse herself and, going in
search of him, encounters the night watchman, who
beats her. This highly suggestive passage tells us something about two elements of love: our increased vulnerability once we open ouselves to love and the pre-
cipitous unleashing by love of unknown forces, depicted

here as figures of the night. An analogous incident occurs in Exodus (4:24):

> At a night encampment on the way, the Lord encountered [Moses] and sought to kill him. So [his wife] Zipporah took a flint and cut off her son's foreskin and touched his legs with it, saying, "You are truly a bridegroom of blood to me!" And when He let him alone, she added, "A bridegroom of blood because of the circumcision."

No further reference is made to this incident, just as no further reference is made in the Song of Songs to the night visit. In both cases, the text goes on to detail increasing intimacy between the lovers. But if love heals our most essential wounds and deepest flaws, opening ourselves up to love may result, not only in illumination and healing, but also in the terror of facing our flaws. In Moses' view his flaw lay in his identity as one of the Children of Israel. The mark of his identity, which he bore in his own flesh, was passed on to his son by Zipporah's hasty circumcision of the boy.

Moses received an initial call that began the healing of his flawed sense of self. His response to the call was muted temporarily by the nocturnal attack, after which all became well lit and clear once again. Moses grew ever closer to God, and even God's denying him entry into the Promised Land did not stand in the way of their intimacy. Such intimacy, if we achieve it, has nothing to do with getting what we want, as Moses' case clearly shows. Instead, it means experiencing God's presence in everything we do get.

The Children of Israel's Deepening Love of God

The Israelites' experience of God's love was not the same as that of Moses: his was an individual love story.

Similarly, each of us must individually open up to God's love. We are aided in this by the faith and constancy of those around us, but our relationship with God must be entered into, experienced, and maintained individually. While we may be tempted to work through a mediator or find some ritual as a substitute for our own involvement, ultimately we must each make a personal commitment.

At the time of the plagues, the Children of Israel had not yet awakened to God's love. They were going through a stage in which they found and lost belief in rapid succession. When we review Exodus, we look for the point where their awakening occurred, not their obedience to Moses, but their own awakening—when they heard the call, "Arise my darling; my fair one, come away! For now the winter is past, the rains are over and gone. The blossoms have appeared in the land, the time of pruning has come; the song of the turtledove is heard in our land." What we are looking for, then, is the moment when the healing of the Israelites began.

Love healed Moses' deepest wound, his troubled identity, demonstrating love's power to heal. Love is also the source of meaning and of life itself. We can analyze the ten plagues visited on the Egyptians in terms of our model of love. We find that when love is withdrawn, the following things happen. First, we are struck by boils and cattle disease, that is, we lose our source of healing. Second, we are plunged into darkness, symbolically losing our world of meaning. Third, and most vital of all, we lose life itself and the ongoingness of life, symbolized by the deaths of the first-born. All that remains is terror, which is the opposite of love. At the Sea of Reeds, the Israelites faced terror. They had a choice: either they could become paralyzed and drown in terror, or they could be carried through by love.

Our model of love entails aspects of ourselves that we cannot normally accept because we have been loved only conditionally. When someone loves us unconditionally, we, like the beloved in the Song of Songs, can accept our weaknesses: "I am dark but beautiful." We can change our attitudes because we are loved completely, and by accepting our weaknesses we can be healed. We must ask what aspect of themselves the Children of Israel, as a people, disliked, and at what point they sensed that God accepted that aspect.

The Children of Israel were slaves. Though enslavement was inflicted on them from outside, after a while they began to internalize the condition. Instead of forming a positive self-identity, they felt themselves to be victims. Yet it was precisely because of their suffering and outcry that God rescued them and brought them out of Egypt to a land flowing with milk and honey. The rescue played an important part in their healing, but it was not everything. The Israelites had to learn to love themselves and God. It is not enough to reject the identity of a slave. Some positive identity must emerge. A curious passage in the Gospel of John suggests just how complete the Israelites' healing was:

> Jesus said to the Jews who had believed in him, "If you continue in my word, you are truly my disciples, and you will know the truth, and the truth will make you free." They answered him, "We are descendants of Abraham, and have never been in bondage to anyone. How is it that you say 'You will be made free'?" (John 8:31)

The story of the bondage in Egypt and the liberation by God has always been central to Jewish self-understanding. How then could these Jews claim never to have been in bondage, and how could they describe their freedom as resting in their descent from Abraham? The explanation rests on the fact that bondage can be found either in what others do to us or in our selfidentification. Once the Jews had fully claimed God's covenantal relationship with Abraham, their servitude

in Egypt was no longer a wound to their self-understanding, because recognizing a covenant with God is
liberating. So the full healing of their wound entailed
not only their rescue from slavery, but their full acceptance of God's covenant. Their time in the wilderness
was actually spent in pursuit of the latter; they wandered
not for the sake of purgation, purging the attitudes of
slavery, but for the sake of increasing their intimacy
with God.

You may wonder what difference there is between
conceiving of the wilderness years as purgative and
conceiving of them as a time of growing intimacy. We
can draw a distinction between the purgative and intimacy models by looking at the senses of self and God
that each one entails. When we consider Exodus as a
journey, we see ourselves as slaves, sinners, and deficient
beings; God is one who judges, purges, and liberates.
But when we think of the Exodus story as depicting
the deepening love between the Israelites and God, then
we see ourselves as beloved and God as lover. The latter
interpretation does not mean that we are not slaves,
sinners, and deficient beings. It does mean that, before
judging, God loves us and that we experience this love.
The difference between interpretations may seem small,
but it is crucial. God calls us, not by pointing out our
faults, but through love and desire. Because we feel
loved, we are willing to be transformed. We trust the
process and are able to let God into our lives. Once
the love is established, a relationship develops that can
be as demanding as any traditionally associated with
the journey model.

Simone Weil observed, "Hell is a flame which burns
the soul. Paradise also. It is the same flame. But, depending on the orientation of the soul, this single and
unique flame constitutes infinite evil or infinite good."[2]
When an external force causes us to change by destroying some aspect of ourselves or our lives, we feel as

though we were undergoing cruel punishment or even torture. Torture, in fact, can be defined as the re-formation of a person's view of the world through ex-ternal coercion. On the other hand, if we must transform ourselves to get closer to the one we love, we do so willingly and are grateful for any aid we may receive. Whatever stands between us and our beloved becomes hateful and we yearn to have it purged. Therein lies the difference between the two wilderness models: one involves purgation, and the other, deepening love for the beloved.

8. In the Presence of the Flood

What good does it do to look back to Creation to find God's love? After all, God may have loved us in the past, but we are in the present. That is precisely why the Rabbis teach that God renews the work of Creation every day, Creation is present! Thus, the ever-present reality of God's love can renew our world.

We began our exploration with several biblical texts that described past events. We studied these texts in an effort to discover whether there was something in those past events that could nourish and sustain us as we face the ongoingness of time. Our experience of time has included moments of deep pain and disillusionment. Our personal exploration, not unlike the one depicted in David's Psalm 22, grew out of a need to deal with such painful moments.

> My God, my God,
> why have You abandoned me;
> why so far from delivering me
> and from my anguished roaring?
> My God,
> I cry by day—You answer not;
> by night, and have no respite.

But the psalmist looks beyond his own misfortune to the larger story of God's faithfulness to Israel.

> But You are the Holy One,
> enthroned,
> the Praise of Israel.

> In You our fathers trusted;
> they trusted, and You rescued them.
> To You they cried out
> and they escaped;
> in You they trusted
> and were not disappointed.

Viewing time from this larger perspective, the psalmist begins to feel some hope. There is a long history of God's faithfulness. The psalmist can also explore his own history and discover that it, too, is filled with the presence and care of God.

> You drew me from the womb,
> made me secure at my mother's breast.
> I became Your charge at birth;
> from my mother's womb You have been
>   my God.

But the psalmist's current trials intrude on his consciousness.

> Many bulls surround me,
> mighty ones of Bashan encircle me.
> They open their mouths at me
> like tearing, roaring lions.
> My life ebbs away:

But, even then, the psalmist envisions his rescue by God and how the story of that rescue will be joined up with all the earlier accounts of God's faithfulness.

> Deliver me from a lion's mouth;
> from the horns of wild oxen rescue me.
> Then will I proclaim Your fame to my brethren,
> praise You in the congregation.
>
> You who fear the Lord, praise Him!
> All you offspring of Jacob, honor Him!
> Be in dread of Him, all you offspring of Israel!

> For He did not scorn, He did not spurn
> the plea of the lowly;
> He did not hide His face from him;
> when he cried out to Him, He listened.
>
> (Psalm 22)

Past presence becomes warrant for present hope. God was always there for the Children of Israel. God was there in our earlier history. God will again be present.

But surely we have all had past loves that are no longer sustained. Re-reading old love letters can assure us we have been loved, but it cannot lead to the conclusion that we are still loved or will be loved in the future. Regarding this issue, the rabbis insist that our temporal way of thinking has nothing to do with God's sense of time. For God, past, present, and future are simultaneous. If God once loved us, God still loves us. God renews the work of Creation every day. In this way the past is continually present to us and is, in some essential way, our present. This is why the Exodus story is retold, not as an old story that we must remember, but as a current event in which we are the participants. Many exiles, wars, and cruelties have occurred since the Jews were led out of Egypt, yet all these events are somehow aspects of the Exodus.

Comparing our lives to the Exodus story is a reassuring exercise, since Exodus has a positive and uplifting ending. Yet the Exodus story does have its troubling aspects. For instance, if God is perpetually liberating us, God is also forever drowning the Egyptians. Even if we focus on the God of liberation in Exodus, we still must come to understand the God of the Flood.

> Let the faithful exult in glory;
> let them shout for joy upon their couches,
> with paeans to God in their throats
> and two-edged swords in their hands,
> to impose retribution upon the nations,

punishment upon the peoples,
binding their kings with shackles,
their nobles with chains of iron,
executing the doom decreed against them.
This is the glory of all His faithful.
Hallelujah!
(Psalm 149: 5–9)

The Flood

Our study began with the Flood, God's covenant, and Noah's understanding of what he could hope for and expect from the ongoingness of time. Using what we have learned in subsequent chapters, we must now go back and try to discover what was going on during the Flood. If God will always love us, and has always loved us, why did God cause the Flood?

There is a tradition that the chief sin of the generation of the Flood was their refusal to beget children. Even Noah refused to marry and have children. His first child was not born until he was 500 years old! He, too, said: "Why should I bring offspring into a world which will likely be destroyed"?[1] Why was Noah so opposed to having children? In a fascinating discussion of the Kaddish (the prayer recited in memory of the dead) Yaakov Culi explains some of Noah's reluctance. The commentary discusses whether or not it is important to have children who can say Kaddish in order to elevate one's soul after death.

> God does not want anyone to depend on his children. Even in our world, we see that when a person loses his fortune, he is not helped by his children—even though he did many good things for them. How then can one expect his children to help him after he dies? His children will rapidly forget him, and pay no attention to his adverse

situation. As soon as the seven days of mourning are over, they are once again immersed in their affairs, and they no longer even think about the parents who brought them into the world. . . . The Midrash teaches that when a saint's child dies and his eyes brim with tears, God consoles him, "Why are you weeping? If it is because of the fruit that you will not leave in the physical world, behold, you have fruit that is better than children. This fruit consists of the good deeds you have done, the Torah you have studied, and the support you have given to Torah scholars."[2]

There is a marvelous pathos and irony in this passage. God's consolation of his creations when *their* creations go awry occurs in the midst of a commentary on God's creation gone awry.

Salvation through Creation

If our temptation is to not create, salvation comes through creating.

Come and see why did the Holy One blessed be He command Noah to make the ark? In order that mankind should see him engaged in its construction and repent of their ways. Would not the Holy One blessed be He have saved him by His word or have borne him up to Heaven by his faith that He said to him, "Make for thee an ark of gopher wood"? Wherefore thus? But said the Holy One blessed be He: "Since I say to him: 'Make for thee an ark of gopher wood,' and he becomes engaged in the work and cuts cedar wood, they will gather around him and say to him: Noah! What makest thou? Saith he: An ark!— Because God hath told me that He is bringing a deluge on the earth. As a result of this, they will listen and will repent. So the Holy One blessed be He thought . . . but they took no notice."[3]

Nehama Leibowitz, who quotes this midrash, focuses on the building process, which serves as a sign of the impending destruction and allows adequate time for others to repent. As we have seen, the account of the Flood is about creativity and our ambivalence concerning the role of creator, so the construction of the ark is an intrinsically sacramental activity.

There are essentially two forms of creation, one producing a live creature and the other, a dead artifact. The creation that produces a dead artifact is characterized by control and manipulation. No matter how skillfully it is done, the deadness remains. Living creation always involves giving and emptying of the self, with a concomitant loss of control. In order for the creature to be alive, it must be free. However, what we give away may be returned to us as a gift from our creation.

Giving birth to a child is an emptying of the self. Until its birth, the child is completely ours, bone of our bone, flesh of our flesh. At the moment of birth, the separation begins. As life goes on the gap becomes ever wider. In an attempt to hold onto our creation, we may try to restrict the ways in which the child grows. But you cannot simultaneously give a gift and hold onto it. If we really give the gift of life to our offspring, we give it to them to use or even abuse. Reaching out to another in love is also an emptying of the self and relinquishing of control. The resulting relationship is also an independent creature. We can try to control it, or we can sense its life and let it lead us where it will. Thus, self-emptying and relinquishing of control is the form of creation that takes us beyond control and mere technique. Its source may be found in the fact that we are created in the image of God, who gave us freedom. Living creation grows out of love and delight. This is the sunny side of the street.

But this discussion of creativity would not be complete without dealing with the concept of creation gone awry and its subsequent destruction. We have always known there was a dark side of creation, a memory we might not wish to explore. Creativity is not just a wonderful thing, it is also an awful thing. Imagination is not only the vestibule of the Holy of Holies, it is also the vestibule of the demonic. "Who forms light and creates darkness, who makes peace and creates all things." The Isaiah quotation actually ends with the words, "creates evil," but when the rabbis inserted the quotation in the morning prayer service they amended it to "all things," feeling that the creation of evil was too difficult a truth to face in the early morning hours. We know that it is creative to put paint on a canvas. We must also recognize that creativity can be involved in removing paint from a canvas. Creativity is part of pruning as well as of growth.

Creation and destruction are not simply opposites. Destruction is an essential aspect of the creative process. Earlier we gave the example of the surgeon who cuts away diseased tissue to save an otherwise healthy organ. We are justifiably repelled by the idea of cutting away aspects of a people in order to purify the remnant, which was attempted after the Babylonian exile. But our perspective needs to be ahistorical. We are not really asking what *was* going on during the Flood, but what *is* going on during the Flood. If we consider Creation to be ongoing, then the Flood is also ever present. We have discussed the constant renewal of bondage and liberation, but we have not yet considered examples illustrating the ongoingness of the Flood.

Last year I moved my study from the first floor to the second. The process was far more complex than that simple description suggests. It required opening a closet piled high with papers, pulling out the fruit cartons used as filing cabinets, and examining their contents. In the end, I filled eight large trash bags with papers. I wish I could say I was relieved when the work was done. Actually, I was horrified! I had published three books, but I discovered that I had written *seven*. Each of those seven books entailed a forest's worth of wood pulp in typing paper. For every line in the published books, it seemed I had "unwritten" three. I felt despair when I saw those trash bags on the curb. Years of my life and thought discarded, wasted effort. But that reaction was a false one. The writing was not done just to produce books, it was also a way of thinking. The rewriting and discarding of earlier writings were a kind of rebuke and judgment, which are as important to creation as loving-kindness and compassion.

It is one thing to talk about piles of discarded paper but quite another to deal with discarded lives. Floods are the destruction of life as we know it, or at least of the structures that give life meaning and value. Often, the flood we must face is personal. Consider an example of such a personal catastrophe. Young and strong, full of dreams of the future, we are suddenly informed that we must undergo surgery to remove a malignant tumor. We are also told that the cancer may have spread. We ask ourselves, how could all our dreams have been so quickly and cruelly wiped out? How could God allow such an event? We are asking the wrong questions. They are the wrong questions, not because they are unanswerable or because we are uncomfortable with the answers, but because such questions misconstrue what is actually happening. We function in time; hence, it makes sense for us to think in terms of causality. In our experience cause generally precedes effect. But God, as we have said, is outside of time. Therefore, the notion of causality is inapplicable when we think about God. The appropriate question is, "What can I do with what has been given to me?" The cynical response, to refuse to accept it, will not do. Floods are not stayed by nonacceptance. With or without our acceptance, the waters climb and wash away a good part of our world. If, instead, we confront tragedy and begin rebuilding our lives, we are participating in the most significant form of creativity.

We brought to the Noah Paradox our creativity, spirituality, and love. But we must realize more completely what these concepts mean. To fully understand them is to recognize that destruction is inherent in all three ways.

Spirituality and Destruction

We've already discussed the destructive side of spirituality. That is the purpose of the purgative stage of the journey. Aspects of the self must be gradually purged so that the unsullied self can emerge. The years that the Children of Israel spent in the wilderness constitute a time of purgation, a pruning back. In that environment, away from other cultural symbols, they were purged of the habits of slavery and the values they had unconsciously picked up in Egypt. We've talked about the paring away of the accretions that are the result of living unthinkingly. The symptom of such paring away may be sorrow. But if we are committed to the process of transformation, we can experience the sorrow as a joyous sign that change is taking place. Such a transformation occurs within a woman in labor. Her focus is not on the contractions as pain but as signs that she is about to give birth. If someone were to offer to remove the contractions but also the unborn child, she would not accept. Similarly, if we know that sorrow is but a symptom of the birth of something new, we can rejoice as sorrow increases in intensity, because we are eagerly looking forward to a new life. The sorrow is brought on not only by the pain of bearing new life, but also as a sort of mourning for the aspect of ourselves that is dying.

Spirituality has traditionally meant a way to relate to God or reality. Zen Buddhism teaches that there are many Ways. "What are called the Ways are fractional expressions of Zen in limited fields such as the fighting arts of sword or spear, literary arts like poetry or calligraphy, and household duties like serving tea, polishing, or flower arrangements. These actions become Ways when practice is done not merely for the immediate results but also with a view to purifying, calming, and focusing the psycho-physical apparatus, to attain to some degree of Zen realization and express it."[4] This insight, that diverse practices can help realize a common fundamental spiritual truth, is not limited to Zen. In our attempt to relate more closely to God, we too have several ways open to us. One of them is the way of love. Love can be a way when it entails the right type of desire.

Spirituality and Desire

Desire is basic to human nature and to our lives: desire to live, to continue to live. Fear constricts desire; in fact, it is a kind of negative desire (fear of nonexistence, of death, of isolation). Desire has a far greater force than fear.

The radical differences in attitudes toward desire among different religions suggest that desire is a concept that needs careful examination. In the West, desire has been understood to be our life energy. It is generally believed to be the cause of our actions. In Eastern thought, desire is the cause of all suffering and sorrow. The extinction of desire is the goal.

Desires are distinguished by their objects. With some objects of desire, reaching the goal does not satisfy the desire. In such cases, when we achieve what we longed for, we realize that that was not the actual object of our desire. We are still dissatisfied. The second kind of desire works like a chain reaction. At first we want a roof over our head. After we get the roof, we begin to long for walls and a floor. After we complete the structure, our desires turn to furnishings. Such desires can go on and on. There is a third kind of desire. It, too, is never fully satisfied. It continually increases, yet the desire *is* the satisfaction. Rather than the emptiness that comes with desiring something that proves not to be *it* when you get it, or the desires that constantly lead to further desires, this desire is a deepening of our relation to the mystery surrounding us.

The goals of the three types of desire outlined above can be labeled intrinsic, mixed, or instrumental goals. Say that we enjoy walking. Walking can be an intrinsic goal, if we love it for itself; or, it can be a mixed goal if it becomes a way to get where we want to go. But once we focus on the goal of arriving at a place, the walking becomes an instrumental goal. When this happens, walking becomes less and less pleasurable. By focusing on the end of the process, we have turned the formerly pleasurable process into a burden. So the choice of certain types of goals can reduce large parts of our lives to instrumental processes, destroying much of the pleasure that can be obtained from everyday activities.

It is true that desire does not motivate every act. We sometimes act purely out of an abundance of energy. For instance, we may walk down the street singing. We may be walking because we have to get somewhere, but we are probably singing out of sheer energy and joy. But could this energy which leads us to bound up the stairs two at a time, be adequate to explain the motivation of an entire life? Only desire is that powerful and all-encompassing. One of the profound insights of Buddhism is its concentration on desire. Desire is a problematic force, one that is at the root of most of our suffering as well as most of our actions. But whether the route to serenity and understanding is through the *extinction* of desire or the *transformation* of desire is a point on which Western thought disagrees with Eastern. The problem for us in the West is not whether or not to desire. Desire is our life energy; we *must* desire. The problems are *what* to desire and *how* to desire.

Say we have a desire to write the great American novel. This is an unexamined desire, and, as such, its goal is unclear. Do we desire the fame and credit for writing the great American novel? If so, our desire will probably lead to frustration. We do have control of our writing, but not of fame. To desire fame is to give control of our desires to people with mixed motives. But perhaps our desire is not for fame or credit but for the joy of being able to find the right word, the correct confluence of meaning and sound. Then what we are searching for is not an end but a process that puts us in touch with what is beautiful and true. In this case, the daily struggle with the blank paper, as we have already remarked, is not to draw out something beautiful, or to make a name for oneself, but a way of relating to reality, which is the third type of desire. This type of desire is free from suffering. Because the desiring itself is intrinsically good, because the desire is the satisfaction, it is possible to desire without suffering.

The key for an activity's becoming a way seems to lie in the type of desire that motivates it. Thus, love can become a way when what began as love for a particular person opens up, in Dante's words, to "the love that moves the sun and other stars." Creativity can become a way when its object becomes not fame or even the creation but the process that allows one to relate to the creative source. Literary arts, plastic arts, all artistic endeavors in general can certainly be ways. Household duties, especially the duty of caring for children, spouse, aging parents, or others, can also be ways.

Love and Destruction

Must love entail destruction? Love seems to start off so simply with attraction and desire. Yet, as we have discussed, desire is not simple. "Whenever one loves a person, it seems, one also is likely to hate that person; for whenever a person can cause great joy in one's life he can also cause great pain and usually does, and so he becomes simultaneously the object of hope and disappointment, of confidence and of fear, of trust and of mistrust, of affection and of resentment."[5] But the terms we are relating are not love and hate, but love and destruction. Destruction frequently occurs because of hatred, but not exclusively so. Destruction *can* occur because of love. This destruction, as we will see below, is the destruction of projections that obscure the reality of the beloved.

Love has been defined by Spinoza as joy with the idea of an external cause. He further defines joy as the movement from a lesser to a greater perfection. This definition expresses an expansive notion of love. Love is not a state, it is a process, a movement. This movement is not obsessive but expansive. By this definition a love that reduces the world to the dyadic relationship of lover and beloved is not love. Love should open up the entire world to us, increase our sympathy and compassion, and increase our knowledge. As insightful and profound as Spinoza's definition is, it seems to work best as a tool for ruling out what is *not* love. For instance, we can rule out obsessions, because they reduce our world. But Spinoza suggests that love is a response to something we see as an external cause. Of course we don't just love those who love us, but something in the other is, according to Spinoza, the trigger of the love. But is there no love outside the domain of causality? Can't love just well up from within us, not because of an external cause, but because of an internal fullness?

That would remove love from Spinoza's catalogue of emotions or passions and treat it as an action. Marion Milner suggests that love is actually a form of creativity, one we deceive ourselves in not acknowledging; "when in love one can struggle against knowing that the miraculous quality is something one is oneself creating."[6]

Jacob didn't simply teach Leah to love Rachel and his sons, he taught her what it was to love someone who rejected her. It was a lesson she might have preferred not to learn, yet an invaluable lesson if one wants to be capable of joy. Such love is free. It is not changed by a moment's glance, a smile, or a frown—it flows regardless of pain. Indeed, the object of our love must itself be free. It must be beyond our control—even unpredictable—and thereby be capable of surprising us. As Jacob discovered, people can love God because they cannot control God.

The Death of Love

Our capacity to love is a gift from God. All that we love is an irradiation from God. Nevertheless, sometimes it is counterproductive to focus on God as a way to know God. Sometimes we can sense God more clearly when we focus on other people and on loving them fully. As we open to them, we become closer to God than if we turned away from them and tried to come into God's presence directly.

We first discover the love of God in and through the love of others. Loving others inevitably involves the loss of love. Love may be fiercer than death, but the loss of love is a kind of death. The loss can occur so mysteriously, so gradually. In the face of the loss of a human love, can we still believe in and discover a transcendent love? The traditional Jewish model of the relationship between God and the Jewish people was the model of courtship, love, marriage, unfaithfulness, reconciliation, and renewed covenant. But as twentieth-century people we know that unfaithfulness does not always allow for reconciliation; that courtship may bespeak lust, rather than love; and that over time love may not only weaken and fail, it may actually die. The Song of Songs affirms, in the face of the death of the beloved, that love is fiercer than death. The problem we are trying to solve is not the death of the beloved, but the death of love itself. And yet, in such cases, is it love that is lost or just the *object* of that love? Once love has been awakened and the self has been liberated from slavery to its own narrow interests, the awakening remains even when the object is no longer loved. The transformation that love engendered is real and is not lost when love is gone. All we have loved changes us, re-creates us. The death of love is as real and as wrenching as the death of a beloved. But the insight that love is fiercer than death holds for the death of love as well as for the death of the beloved. What we have learned through love remains with us.

Transformation

The time after the Flood is not Creation but re-creation. "In understanding God's ultimate purpose in creating, we usually think in terms of two models, either that of destruction and creation anew, or that of transformation of the existing creation."[7] Earlier, in discussing the fear of nothing and nothingness, we saw that the fear was about whether or not our worlds of meaning and value are grounded in a larger reality. Are they based on something or nothing? But there is another fear of nothing. As we move through different periods in our life, we wonder whether or not we retain something from our earlier dreams and aspirations, or

whether we are always building anew. Is the process of
moving on one of discarding and outgrowing, or one
of refining an essential aspect that grows increasingly
pure? Do we disown the explorer, the digger of holes,
the climber of trees that we were at age six, or do we
recognize that same curiosity we had then, now shaped
and refined over our lifetime? Destruction or transformation? The destruction of the Flood can be reconceived
as transformation.

If we view the Flood as transformation, not destruction, we have found a solution to the Noah Paradox.
That is, the problems may be recurrent, but *we are new!*
In Genesis, Noah is told how to build the ark and
which animals to put into it. But there is much more
preserved in the ark than the animals. Remember that
the end of the Flood is not Creation but re-creation.
Much is preserved within Noah's ark. For instance, the
concept of limit is preserved. Limit transforms chaos to
cosmos. Time is one kind of limit, but limit in its
generic form is part of the creative force. For example,
it is the limit on the waters that keeps back the Flood.
It is the limit on our life expectancy that makes us post-
Flood humans. (Tradition holds that, prior to the Flood,
there was no natural life expectancy. People died of
accidents and murder, but not of aging.) Into the ark
goes all that is essential for creating, because what is
essential to this process will remain essential. We could
return to Genesis 1 in order to find out which things
from the first days of creation were *not* destroyed in the
flood: light and the lesser lights (sun, moon, and stars).
But there is another approach. Suppose we are told that
our world will be destroyed, but we will be preserved.
After the destruction, we will have the task of recreating
our world. We are given time, but a very limited space,
to collect those things that will be necessary for the re-
creation of our world. Part of our task in gathering
those things necessary for re-creation is the imperative

not to include anything that led to the flaw resulting in the destruction. We must create again, but we must not simply duplicate a faulty world.

In small ways our worlds shift, are overturned, are destroyed. We move, we lose our jobs, aging changes our status and our concerns. During each flood, we hold on to those items that will enable us to continue and to rebuild. We fashion our own arks to help us preserve these essentials.

> Certainly religious meaning cannot be contained in a box, but the "box" is an admission that meaning "shows itself" in our lives. The box may be—larger than a breadbox, even the breadbox itself—the resting place of the host; it may be a room, a house, a cathedral, or the City of God or the Vision of Heaven. Some of the boxes that will draw our attention already have been perceived as containers of the sacred; others are the boxes that anyone except the owner, and perhaps even the owner, would say contain junk. These are the sacred possessions opaque to all but the memory of the owner. These are the things that are thrown out when people move, die, go to college, or change their minds about who they are. The box may be anything from Nicholas of Cusa's mystical circle to a map of the universe, from a cartoon to a kiss, from an aquarium to a quilt.[8]

Another way of exploring what is preserved after a Flood is to see what of human nature remains after the devastation of neurological disorder. Oliver Sacks's case studies show the ark of cosmos floating over the chaos of neurological disturbance. Sacks convincingly shows that the order of what it is to be human is retained even after the flood of memory loss or the loss of the sense of physical identity due to loss of proprioception. He deals with the chaos arising from lack of limit, as in the cases of a man with Tourette's syndrome and a woman with *tabes dorsalis*. The only person he finds who has not retained what was essential for re-creating after the flood is Dr. P., who has lost what was intuitive, personal, comprehensive, and concrete.[9] In discussing the man whose memory was lost due to Korsakov's syndrome, Sacks quotes A. R. Luria: "A man does not consist of memory alone. He has feeling, will, sensibility, moral being. . . . It is here . . . you may touch him, and see a profound change."[10]

So it is clear that in our ark we must preserve feeling (although we are tempted to numbness after the devastation), will (although passivity lures us), sensibility, and moral being.

The problem that we have been dealing with is that if creativity is present, so is destruction; if spirituality and love are present, so are estrangement and absence. In our quest for a way to confront the dark side of our experience, we found that it is desire that determines whether something does or does not become a way. The third kind of desire, desire that is itself a form of satisfaction, allows us to experience the Flood, not as destruction, but as transformation. This new appraisal of the Flood is the beginning of our response to the Noah Paradox.

9. Destruction Reconsidered

To finally resolve the Noah Paradox, we must somehow reconceive suffering, not as punishment, but as a transformative way. This is the understanding offered by Rabbi Akiba. Instead of being punishment for sin, suffering is an occasion to offer up our love to God. In order to discuss suffering, we should not talk about sin, or good and evil, in any simplistic sense. That is not to say that the concept of suffering extends beyond good and evil, but good and evil are not what suffering is about. Simone Weil said that there is nothing more boring than evil; she is right. Read twenty murder mysteries in rapid succession, or daily newspaper headlines, and you will discover (if you don't already know it) that evil is repetitive, boring, and unimaginative. But neither is good very interesting, at least as it is commonly understood. To most people, "good" usually means little more than the absence of evil, much as "peace" is the absence of war. Peace, in reality, is much more than the absence of war, but we have failed to name that "much more." And good, in reality, is much more than not doing wrong or even doing right, but we haven't spelled that out fully either.

Suppose we spend our childhood trying to be a *good* pianist. We try to practice the way a *good* student might. A good student would count every beat and curve her fingers. We are tempted to race through the passages we know and love, looking for the music behind the notes, and stumbling over the passages we have not yet learned. Instead, we practice methodically, the way a good student might, hoping to become a good pianist.

We have forgotten that there is no one listening. We
will not win favor or love by our way of playing. No
one cares if we curve our fingers, remember to count,
or slip into our own passionate and erratic way of
playing. Yet to learn to be a pianist, one does have to
curve one's fingers, count beats, and practice scales and
arpeggios. But the curved fingers, the counting, the
scales are boring, especially to others, as our neighbor's
noisy closing of her windows reminds us. Of course we
need technique, but technique is not an end in itself;
it is only useful for producing music. We also need
virtue. But virtue is a necessary, not a sufficient condition for art or life. If our sole objective in life is to
never cause any pain, never make any thoughtless re-
mark, and never take any indelicate action, we should
simply die as soon as possible. We can see that simply
not doing evil is not what virtue is about. Doing evil
prevents us from making music in the same way that
poor technique prevents us from making music. Good
is really about making music. What music? What is the
source of our song?

> As kingfishers catch fire, dragonflies draw flame;
> As tumbled over rim in roundy wells
> Stones ring; like each tucked string tells, each hung
>   bell's
> Bow swung finds tongue to fling out broad its name;
> Each mortal thing does one thing and the same:
> Deals out that being indoors each one dwells;
> Selves—goes itself; *myself* it speaks and spells,
> Crying *What I do is me: for that I came*.[1]

So peace is not the absence of war. Rather, war
obstructs peace; it prevents the warring parties from
becoming what they most truly are. Nor is good the
absence of evil. Good is the full expression of what we
most essentially are. So the true vision of the peaceable
kingdom is *not* the vision of the lion lying next to the

lamb. In a true state of peace, a lion must be a lion, and a lamb must be a lamb; and a lamb lying next to a lion will soon be devoured.

Therefore, our purpose is to be ourselves. Evil is that which stands in the way of our full being. Whatever is, is good. "By reality and perfection I understand the same thing."[2] That is why, as each word God utters in Genesis 1 becomes reality, God could repeatedly see "that it was good." Being is good. Evil is impediment, diminishment, constriction, and negation.

The Self and Suffering

The starting point for seeking good in our lives is an awareness of the distinction between appearance and reality. Reality, not appearance, equals perfection. The quotation in the previous paragraph is related to another of Spinoza's statements: "The chief good is that [the individual] should arrive, together with other individuals if possible, at the possession of . . . knowledge of the union existing between the mind and the whole of Nature."[3] With an awareness of the union between the mind and nature comes an awareness that we have, up to now, identified with an apparent self rather than our real self. Our *real* self is undivided, undamaged, and free from suffering. If in the past we have identified with our apparent, rather than our real, self, we have experienced the suffering caused by false identification. We have said that destruction is inherent in creativity, spirituality, and love. The destruction is the cutting away of that which is not real but only apparent.

We don't know who we are. We don't know who God is, perhaps because we don't know ourselves. When we say that we want to know who God is, we think that the unknown in that statement is "God." We don't realize that we are as unknown to ourselves as God is.

Any light shed on either of these unknowns also illuminates the other. Hence, if we learn more about our real self, we will also know a little more about God.

The pianist Artur Rubinstein was asked what he thought about while performing. He responded that he thought about the bagel and lox he was going to eat after the concert. In other words he was keeping his apparent self occupied and out of the way so that his real self, the part of him that knew the music and had learned every aspect of it, would be free to perform without the interference of his apparent self. I have used this insight in a more ignoble way. I am a poor tennis player. But if I get annoyed after losing point after point to my opponent's superior serve, I simply tell my opponent how impressed I am with her serve and ask her how she does it. She invariably misses the next serve. The apparent self that is conscious, that counts beats and curves fingers, that concentrates on the movement of the racquet, must be left behind when we are ready to really make music or play tennis.

These examples give us a clue to our mystery, but only a small one. They don't take us very far toward an understanding of the real self. They do suggest that the real self is not focused on an external standard of judgment. For the real self to emerge, the audience, whether critical or appreciative, must disappear. As long as we are aware of being viewed and judged, our real self remains hidden. Although it may seem contradictory to say that the real self emerges in moments of self-forgetfulness, the statement is nonetheless true and reminds us of our experiences. There are moments of extreme grief or crisis, of great joy, or just ordinary life, when we finally get out of our own way and experience the world directly. During those moments, even those involving grief or crisis, we sense what is meant by "God saw that it was good."

We are constantly building. We build selves, roles, and scenarios. How can we tear down these false fronts to reveal the real self behind the scenes? For some, meditation or religious devotion is the way. Frequently, it is not we who tear down the false fronts, but some major event, such as aging, illness, or loss. Here we confront the destructive component in creativity, spirituality, and love: the tearing away of the false self to get at the real self.

Another way of understanding this destructive component is in terms of the concept of surrender to the "Other." In the ways of love and spirituality, we are clearly dealing with the Holy or wholly Other. This is no less true in the creative way: we are not fashioning things just to satisfy our own desire. We are also opening ourselves to an insistent, "other" reality. What we are looking for in all three ways is something that is real and alive. "All real living must involve a relationship, recurrent moments of surrender to the 'not-self.'"[4] The amazing thing is that it is more important that we reach reality than that we get what we immediately desire. "I had become utterly glad for everything to be as it was; just because it was not what I had pictured, it had a newness that no mere realization of desire could possibly reach."[5]

As an example of surrender to the Other, consider the story of Job. Job knew God was God. But he didn't know what it was to *be* God. He could repeat everything ever said about God: that God was all-powerful, Creator of heaven and earth. But those words didn't mean anything beyond the conventional ways of talking about God. For Job, God could have been Job's way of facing loneliness or anguish. But one day, God didn't do Job's bidding. Suddenly, God was real! God was not *Job's* creation; Job was *God's*! Job became afraid. But struggling to see beyond his fear, he continued his challenge to God. As a reward, God showed Job God's masterpiece, the whole of creation. Before a consummate artist, one can only express awe and gratitude. Job did both and God was satisfied.

Quest for the Real

We search for living reality. We do not want to love illusions, worship projections, or create dead artifacts. But this quest for reality seems to require the destruction of the unreal or only apparently real. The destruction of apparent reality is experienced as a kind of death, depending on how much we have identified with it. But gradually we come to trust this process of destruction leading to discovery. "The moment of blankness and extinction was the moment of incipient fruitfulness, the moment without which the invisible forces within could not do their work."[6]

The destruction in love is the stripping away of the projections inherent in the early stages of a relationship. "They [the lovers] do not see each other as they really are, but through a rosy haze of emotion which is generated largely by their own inner needs and inadequacies. Each partner appears to the other far more admirable than is really the case." Although the destruction may sometimes be painful, it does not always invalidate the initial bond between a couple. "They have not, as yet, come to distinguish the superficial from the essential, the transitory from the permanent [or as we would say, the apparent from the real]. They think that their 'love' is this heady emotional intoxication that sets their senses reeling; they do not, as yet, understand love as knowing and accepting each other for what they really are, as giving, as sacrifice, as remaining faithful in the face of difficulties and disappointments."[7]

We must go through a similar process of stripping away illusion to understand the reality of God. The end point of this process yields "not God as conscience, parent, authority, but God as experience."[8] If we have previously understood God to be the guarantor of our security, happiness, and well-being, then our first experience of serious loss or tragedy will carry with it not only its own difficulties, but the sense that we have lost God. In fact, we haven't lost God, because we never *had* God. God as wish-fulfiller or Santa Claus has never been met with in experience. Martin Buber has stated that "God" cannot be spoken of, only spoken *to* in prayer. There is an important insight in this statement. The real God is the God we have truly *met*, or understood. But false pictures of God can obstruct our understanding. Consider al-'Alawi's aphorism: "Whoso setteth out for God reacheth him not, but whoso leaneth upon him for support is not unaware of him."[9] In other words, the active search for God must inevitably be unsuccessful, because it is based on some preconceived idea of "God." Leaning on God, on the other hand, is not based on any concept, but on openness to what is. We may lean on God in just those moments when our earlier conception of God has been destroyed, but we find, nonetheless, the strength to go on.

The process of destruction leading to discovery can be found in the story of the Children of Israel. Their earlier concept of God had to do with land, victory, resplendent Temple services, and the royal line of David. They didn't actually *define* God in those terms, but there was a close enough association between God and these elements that with the Babylonian exile, the siege of Jerusalem, the destruction of the Temple, all the earlier notions of God were called into question and ultimately transformed or discarded. Something powerful emerged, powerful enough to endure.

The stripping away that is essential for *real* love to emerge and *real* spirituality to be formed is also required for *real* creativity as well.

> How curious this process of writing is, I must have no enthusiasm, no pride in whether I can do it. There seems always to be a feeling of futility, that I have nothing to say, and usually I try to get away from this by force, by looking for something to say, and then my head begins to ache; but if I accept this futility, give up my purpose to write, and yet don't run away into some other activity, just sit still and feel myself to be no good—then the crystallization begins—after the corruption, blackness, despair.[10]

Destruction is inherent in creativity, spirituality, and love; but we accept and love the destruction for the sake of discovering reality. If the sacrifice involved is forced upon us, it is not sacrifice, but assault and robbery. Love is what makes possible the acceptance of the darkness, confusion, and disruption. Because we love, we can progress in spite of fear. Fear does not detain us. Our love is stronger than our fear. With that in mind, we can reexamine what is going on in creation (ours and God's), what is going on at the Flood (ours and God's), and the love that lifts up and enfolds the whole.

Floods and Creativity

Creation is a gift of love. As we have discussed, creation requires limitation, not only because of the nature of the medium, but also because of the nature of the self. The self must be restrained in creation. We give of ourselves, but we must not impose ourselves on our creation. What fearsome limitation this is! What we create is bone of our bone, flesh of our flesh, and yet it must also be free. We dare not coerce our creation.

We have created that which is alive and necessarily other.

Destruction, as typified by the Flood, is an essential part of the three transformative ways. When we are searching for true understanding, however excellent our first approximation is, it is only an approximation. We learn all we can, retain that which is worth retaining, and discard that which is not worth saving. The discarding feels like death. We worked so hard. Surely we can prop up the weak part of our concept. Must we really prune back to the bare bones? To avoid such difficulties, many people simply reject the idea of Floods. The concepts that result are stunted and ill-formed. In the Middle East, the annual flood of the Nile helps make the land fertile. This kind of flood is essential to our own creative fertility as well. From time to time, our familiar landmarks must be covered over, and all the rules of our world must be challenged. Such floods are not mere exercises, nor do they represent a discipline. A true Flood is an agonizing event. We rarely choose it; more often, we suffer it. Yet, as the following example shows, such suffering leads to true understanding.

> One day the sun didn't shine. The blue turned purple, the green drab. One night the seas raised their heads, bared their fangs, and ate most of my world. In the morning I was alone and wept at my aloneness. I turned to the world and you were there. You were part of a gentler sun. I couldn't see you diffused at first, but you were there in a thousand days, and sung in a thousand songs. And I was no longer alone, so I wept.[11]

The Floods that are part of love can seem to eat up most of our world. But love is fiercer than death. After the waters abate, we begin the slow process of recovering that which was lost and now reappears, transformed. Shakespeare expressed this concept beautifully:

Full fathom five thy father lies,
Of his bones are coral made:
Those are pearls that were his eyes:
Nothing of him that doth fade,
But doth suffer a sea-change
Into something rich and strange.[12]

Losses are real but not final. Atop each flood floats an ark, preserving that which is real. It is difficult at the time to recognize that the loss is not final. But gradually we come to recognize that "nothing of him that doth fade, but doth suffer a sea-change."

We have said that we can accept the destruction inherent in creativity, spirituality, and love, for the sake of the discovery of reality. It is only through such destruction that we can learn to love reality, hence God. But can we love God? Can Noah? What does it *mean* to love God? "Whoso setteth out for God reacheth him not, but whoso leaneth upon him for support is not unaware of him." God is found through intense relationships, not through intellectual pursuit. However, we often hate as well as love the God we find, just as we might both hate and love people: "Whenever one loves a person, it seems, one also is likely to hate that person; for whenever a person can cause great joy in one's life he can also cause great pain and usually does, and so he becomes simultaneously the object of hope and of disappointment, of confidence and of fear, of trust and of mistrust, of affection and of resentment."[13] This process of loving and hating God, of trusting and feeling resentment, is part of the process of stripping away false projections and coming closer to reality. The problem is not that we hate God, but that we don't know God or are indifferent to God. If we hate God, we are already in a relationship with God, a relationship that is full of conflict and tension, like Jacob's. However, out of this conflict will emerge love, not illusion.

Suppose Noah had understood and gone through the process described. Suppose he had recognized, acknowledged, and truly understood the role of destruction in creation. As he stepped out of the ark and surveyed the ravaged earth, his thoughts might have run as follows:

So God had let him win. True, the sheep had died. His sons might not make it to old age. But, holding his wife and watching the sun rise over the remnant of the decimated flock, he loved God.

10. The One Essential Story

In the preceding chapters, we have explored the role of destruction in creativity, spirituality, and love. We have shown that Exodus can be understood as either a journey or a story of deepening love. We have seen how taking the stories of the Exodus and the Flood out of their temporal contexts changes our notion of causality and makes the stories contemporaneous. Given the confluence of creativity, spirituality, and love, we can see that Exodus *is* the story of the Flood told from a different perspective. In both cases something is destroyed and something else is lovingly preserved. We are both those drowned in the Flood and those preserved in the ark. And we ourselves are constantly destroying and creating, building up and tearing down.

We are accustomed to viewing these two stories in radically different ways. The story of the Flood belongs to primordial history. It precedes the singling out of an entire people to form a covenant with God. It is the story of creation gone awry. In contrast, the Exodus story belongs to a more recent historical time. The covenant is presupposed. It is the story of God's action within "modern" history, a story of liberation.

Recorded history is real, but it is not the ultimate reality. We study Exodus, not because it tells us about the past, but because it shows us the deepest meaning of the present. On one level, we would like to distinguish the God of the Flood from the god who liberates us and loves us. However, deep down, we know that God is God is God. And if we are to make sense of the

Exodus story, it must be made consistent with the story of the Flood.

But if the Exodus story *is* the story of the Flood, *both* must also be different formulations of the Song of Songs. In the latter story, destruction comes as a flame of passion, burning away illusions. Depending on our attachment to these illusions, we feel the flame either as tortuous or as warming. As the illusions burn away, new powers emerge within us. Sometimes we experience these powers in terms of creativity, sometimes in terms of spirituality, and sometimes, as pure love.

One Essential Story

The preceding discussion suggests that there is only *one* essential story. At different points in our lives we describe this story differently: as a story of creativity, with God as the master to whom we are apprenticed; as a story of spirituality in which we learn to perceive the sacred in and through the secular; or as a story of deepening love, in which we finally learn total trust. All of the stories central to Western religious tradition can be read in these distinct ways. We tend to choose one way as being more appropriate for a particular story than another. So, for example, we tend to understand the Flood in terms of flawed creativity. But if we are at a point in our lives in which our concentration is on love, the story of the Flood becomes the story of God's tender care, as God selects us out of all creation to receive this care. If we view the story in this way, our world is reduced to a lonely ark floating atop chaos, a powerful image of the intensity of awakened love, a topic we will discuss next.

The Flood of Awakened Love

In the first dawning of love, we tend to find all meaning and value in our beloved. An adolescent girl

I know wrote in her journal, in anticipation of the impending departure of her first love:

> I cannot see beyond the day when you'll be leaving. It is too unreal. You are reality and without you I cannot think. I cling to your thoughts as something stable, unchanged by minutes' actions, but something large and filled with wisdom. And as I close my eyes to see more clearly, the mounting thoughts try to flood my mind. You are reality! And I toss away all thoughts as unrelated. So how can I see or believe in your departure? After you these thoughts will deluge my brain and rise around me. And fighting back these overwhelming thoughts, where will you be? You who are my reality.[1]

The excerpt illustrates the narrow focus of awakened love, typified by the single ark in the Flood story. Just as the destruction of the Flood leads to Noah's awakened love, so too does destruction play an important role in awakened love for everyone who experiences it. The person who has experienced love sees the world in an entirely different way than she did before. Her previous world has been destroyed. The adolescent journal writer tried to reflect in a quieter moment on her twelve-year-old self, the self that existed before she experienced flood of love.

> When curly winds
> Circled over gray clouds' smoke
> I was walking
> Chewing timothy grass
> Picking buttercups;
> I was walking,
> bare feet cool
> on moistened clover,
> looking for a four-leaf one,
> tossing others round;
> I was walking,
> reaching for an apple bough,

over. The year of special intimacy, during which Noah floated in the ark above the floods, was ending. Humdrum dailiness was about to begin. No wonder Noah got drunk! How can we avoid the Noah Paradox? We must make of the ongoingness of time an unambiguous blessing. We must change our daily life by understanding and recognizing our constant relationship with God.

Our new daily life will be like the life of one who has long been married to her beloved. We will get up in the morning and go to work. Perhaps, during the course of the day, we will recall that we are loved. For an instant, we will experience a quiet joy, and then we will return to our task. At the end of the day, we will sit down to eat. Perhaps we will experience the food as a gift, more often we will not notice. As we lie down to sleep, we may feel the joy in resting, or we may just fall asleep. Our covenant with God is everpresent, throughout our day, nourishing and supporting us every moment. It is the single most significant aspect of our life, but we are often unconscious of it. From time to time, we become conscious of it, and with this consciousness come moments of quiet joy and a deep sense of gratitude. From time to time, as in any long marriage, there are disagreements, moments of hurt, even tears. But the trust and faithfulness are stronger than the grief. The grief will be healed, and the love will persist. A Buddhist description of an enlightened person is one who "chops wood and carries water." The tasks of life do not suddenly disappear just because God loves us. In fact, we experience God's love by performing those daily tasks and routines.

The starting point for our search was God's covenant with Noah for the ongoingness of time: "So long as the earth endures, seedtime and harvest, cold and heat, summer and winter, day and night shall not cease." We called this covenant the Noah Paradox because it did not seem like an unambiguous good to Noah. But perhaps we can see it that way, because of what we have learned in the course of our search. Consider the following ambiguous example. Were we sentenced to spend sixty years with a person, seeing him daily, watching him age, sharing meals, it might seem an inhuman punishment. But if we loved that person, the "sentence" would be a wonderful gift.

Living in the daily presence of our beloved, we unconsciously take that presence for granted, but our consciousness of the importance of the beloved quickly returns when this presence is threatened. Suddenly our loved one is ill. We walk so quietly. We try to tempt the sick appetite with tasty food. We spend hours sitting in the same room, hoping to be there when needed. Bringing in a cool glass of water, airing out the room, we feel everything as acts of love. If our loved one recovers, and we have time to reflect, we realize that *all* of our actions, not just those we performed during our beloved's illness, are acts of love. Each day, as we awaken, we become newly aware of the incredible reality of our loved one lying beside us. The separation of sleep allows for the fresh re-creation of that wonder. Usually, though, by the time our morning shower is over, we've forgotten the daily miracle of finding our beloved beside us and are thinking about breakfast. Hence, we must constantly strive to re-create the morning wonder in order to keep our love alive.

The Aging Marriage

And that is how it is with our relationship with God.

This is an incredible statement, that an aging marriage is a metaphor for a life lived with God. Incredible though it may seem, it is repeatedly offered for our consideration throughout the Hebrew Scriptures. For instance, the Israelites' time in the wilderness is called their "bridal days." Our life with God, like theirs, is filled with memories, sweet memories of those early days, sad memories of shared sorrows, and bitter memories of our unfaithfulness. The bitterness has eased as the periods of our faithlessness have receded further and further in time. The pain has become one more shared memory. We look at each other now with deep familiarity, like an old married couple. But the familiarity does not exclude moments of wonder: there will always be the mystery of the other. This aging marriage has bonded us to one who really knows and shares in our every hope, fear, and experience. "God has counted all your tears." God has been with us and for us, through it all. What seemed like a sentence to Noah has become a gift to us.

The Song of Songs seems to be about two young lovers awakening to love. Critics have pointed out that the lovers never talk about having children. In some views, the lack of interest in producing children serves to demonstrate that love is an intrinsic good; hence, procreation is not its ultimate purpose. Yet, when we think about the early days of our love, we remember that we dreamt of seeing that love incarnated in a new life. Perhaps *having* children was not a part of the early years of our love, but dreaming about them was. There is another possible explanation why children are not mentioned in the Song of Songs. Suppose that the lovers are no longer young. Perhaps the couple have already reared their children and are living out the next stage of their life together. But, one might protest, the descriptions of the physical beauty of the lovers belies their age. That is only true if you are not one of the love partners. To one who has grown old with a beloved, their form is a happy conflation of all their expressions, the shyness of youth, the strength of maturity, the vulnerability of age. And the secure tone of the late chapters in the Song of Songs suggests a couple long past childbearing age, whose delight is finally contained totally in each other.

To further support this hypothesis, consider the opening lines of the Song of Songs: "Oh give me of the kisses of your mouth, for your love is more delightful than wine." These words are hardly the greeting of a shy, inexperienced suitor. The text bespeaks a preexisting intimacy, one that is not taken for granted but is being rediscovered. This reawakening to love acts as a renewing force. The woman's response, "I am dark, but comely," reminds us that love doesn't negate reality, but it does allow us to perceive it in a different light. Although we may have liver spots and our hair may be gray and thin, our beloved still looks at us with appreciation. She requests, "Don't stare at me because I am swarthy." In turn, our beloved doesn't stare at us but sees us through the eyes of love, which turn physical imperfections into beloved characteristics.

"Hark! My beloved! There he comes, leaping over mountains, bounding over hills" (2:8). Surely that cannot be said of the aging beloved. Or can it? Consider that this is the same stanza that includes the lines, "Arise, my darling; my fair one, come away! For now the winter is past, the rains are over and gone" (2:10–11). We could interpret this to mean that the lovers have survived winter, the time of loss, separation, and pain. Rains of tears have left them vulnerable. With tenderness, understanding, and an uncertain optimism, the beloved urges the lover to reach out again to life. References to deep, long-term familiarity and respect occur throughout the text: "'Whither has your beloved turned? Let us seek him with you.' My beloved has gone down to his garden, to the beds of spices, to browse in the gardens and to pick lilies. I am my beloved's and my beloved is mine; he browses among the lilies" (6:2–3).

All of this evidence indicates that the Song of Songs can be interpreted as a celebration of the vital role that enduring love plays in our lives. We normally tend to glorify the wonder of new love, an event that is certainly worthy of glorification. But it is enduring love, existing through the years, that allows us to constantly renew the world. Such is God's love for us. Ongoing love is what allows us to finally resolve the Noah Paradox.

11. Conclusion

As a result of our explorations, we have found three related transformative ways: creativity, spirituality, and love. Concerning the first of these, we discovered that creativity is based on the process of self-emptying, giving of oneself for the sake of one's creation. We discussed the courage needed to face the void out of which the creation emerges. We also considered the voluntary limitation of the self needed to allow for the independent life of the creature. We explored the creativity of God, as well as ourselves, when we analyzed Genesis not as historical document but as road map. In doing so, we became more fully aware of the selflessness inherent in genuine creativity. We discovered that this selflessness can, in turn, be understood as both love and spirituality.

Spirituality has been defined as the process of coming into relationship with reality. The goal of this relationship is to teach us to be better lovers. A spiritual person must finally be a loving and creative person. Forming a relationship with reality begins by distinguishing between appearance and reality. Much of the discipline of the spiritual way involves the cutting away of the accretions and appearances that obscure our perception of reality. We approach reality by moving in two complementary directions: inward, to get at our essential self, and outward, to connect with what is around us. The journey within, to discover our essential self, reminds us of the dream journey Ezekiel took in entering the precincts of the Temple of the New Jerusalem. As we renounce that which is not our essential self, we feel some disorientation, as well as some fear. If we peel away all that is not us, will there, in fact, be something that remains?

We learned that love, the third way, is not reducible to a group of feelings. The feelings that frequently accompany love are like the burning bush that accompanied God's revelations to Moses. The feelings are a *sign* of the presence of love but are not in themselves love. Just as spirituality entails a slow transformation of our concept of self, so does love. We gradually move, over our lifetime, from seeking to possess love, to seeking reciprocity in love, to loving regardless of reciprocity, to loving in a way that is deeply caring but nonpossessive. Just as creativity arises out of self-emptying and self-limitation so that the creation can be independent, so love requires our deepest caring, self-giving, and acceptance of the fact that the loved one belongs not to us but to himself or herself. As we fully mature in the way of love, we learn disinterested love, the most difficult, paradoxical, and yet transformative of relationships.

Another connection between these three transformative ways is that each one has a dark side. For example, some artists are cruel and insensitive to others, even though they are exquisitely sensitive to aesthetic nuances. Artists, because they are human, are frequently egocentric. Many intensely spiritual people also become intolerant of others and fanatical in their practices. And many lovers are cruel, because their love is possessive and controlling. Hence, there is a dangerous side to all three ways. In each case, virtue lies in openness, nonpossessiveness, vulnerability, and humility. The dark side emerges when one becomes proud, possessive, and manipulative, losing sight of the real gift and seeking to control the creation. To learn how to care without seeking to control or possess is a difficult lesson. However, if we wish to resolve the Noah Paradox, it is a lesson we must learn and apply to every aspect of our lives.

In our immaturity we constantly seek to control and possess, whether it be through physical manipulation of the environment, political engineering of the state, or rational understanding of the cosmos. But otherness constantly resurfaces, continually interfering with our attempts. Responses to this lack of control vary. We may choose to see it as a problem that we have not yet solved, but one that we will solve, given enough time. We think that we can use engineering, medicine, or logical skills to obtain perfect control. Or, we may deny our lack of control, refusing to see the evidence even as we are confronted by it. Or, we may try to anticipate the worst as a way of regaining partial control. This is the path of doom-sayers.

As we have seen, there is another possible response. Recognizing the limits of our control, we can let go and give way to whatever *is* in control. In doing so, we may discover that lack of control need not be terrifying. The full acceptance of otherness, which includes an acceptance of the lack of control implicit in the independence of the other, is the creative and transformative response to our own limitations. In following this route, we return to the central image of love: the awareness, reverence, and celebration of otherness. Love is the opening of oneself to the other. Love is frightening, for it requires trust and faith, but it is essential for a healthful life. It is valuable in itself, but it is also the direct route to transformation. We must fall in love with our world, with its heartaches, foibles, and injustices; with its people, who suffer and cause suffering; and with the entire panoply of beauty, wretchedness, anguish, compassion, and unexpected moments of grace. Letting go of control, as described herein, is not quietism or indifference. Truly loving the world means being passionately concerned with it. Such a love is active but not controlling, though these two descriptions may seem incompatible. Activity, effort, and discipline are generally considered to be closely related to control. But our experience has shown us that the paradox is only an apparent one. The lives of the artist, the spiritual teacher, and the lover are filled with tremendous energy, effort, and discipline, yet such people's lives are also typified by an openness and sensitivity to an otherness that they cannot control but to which they can respond.

Saints as Artists and Lovers

Let's reconsider the Zen insight about daily activities being acts of love. The followers of Zen have always recognized aesthetic and domestic practices as ways to enlightenment. The time has come for us to claim the same insight. In doing so, we have an opportunity to reconceive our spiritual role models. Traditionally we have thought of them as saints or *tzadikim* or *lamed vavniks*. We may see them now, just as legitimately, as artists or lovers.

Job, for example, has long been described as the paradigmatic saint. God takes and takes and takes, and Job not only accepts but begs God's forgiveness for having questioned the need for such torture. Job's sanctity lies in his abiding faithfulness despite profound suffering. But we can reconceive Job as artist instead of as saint, reading the text with an awareness of God as artist. In fact, that is why artists are sometimes demonic; they are usurping God's role. Only God can see the whole canvas and balance the parts. In this approach, the question at the root of Job's story becomes, Are you safe in the hands of an artist? In this case, feeling safe means that we trust one interpretation of the world more than any other. We believe in the larger design. But if we feel safe in God's hands, are we acting as God *says* or as God *does*? That is, are we God's saints, or, like God, are we artists? Why is Job satisfied at the end of his story? Because Job learns that God is an artist who takes care and pride in creation. Job also learns that *he* is an artist. Job, the artist, is the predecessor both of those who survived the destruction of Jerusalem and of those who survived the Holocaust. Like them, Job must fashion out of aspects of reality a world he can dwell in. What does it mean to Job to be an artist? It means that he can give meaning to what he has suffered, and it is this meaning that enables his survival.

Similarly, suppose we choose to reconceive Abraham, traditionally seen as a saint who accepts whatever God demands of him, even the loss of his son; suppose we were to see him as an artist. Like any genuine artist, Abraham must release his creation to be what it will be, to thrive or to fail. So he approaches Mount Moriah prepared to release his son—perhaps to a fuller life, perhaps to death. How awesome it is to create and then let go. And at the moment of letting go, Abraham, recognizing God's initial artistry, sacrifices with joy and thanksgiving the ram caught in the thicket.

Artists are in constant dialogue with one another. I discovered this when another painter came to look at my father's work. He immediately understood what my father had been trying to do. How lonely my father must have felt when we praised his paintings for the wrong reasons or when we failed to recognize the artistic challenge he had undertaken! Sometimes the public is allowed to hear such dialogue. But the real audience is the fellow artist. How lonely God must have been before Creation. Even now, most of us praise God for the wrong things. We are lacking in true aesthetic sense. To mitigate God's supreme loneliness, God taught Abraham. At last God could have a dialogue. Abraham, my servant, my apprentice, my fellow artist. And later, perhaps in anguish, God taught Job.

So the artist and God are in partnership, although the artist is frequently an unwilling partner. The great artists of Scripture are the "suffering servants." More than any saint, they have taken upon themselves the wrath of God. The three outstanding examples are Abraham, Job, and Hosea. Called "servants of God," they were really God's apprentices. Their artistry and suffering are amazing. And what artifact have they left for us? Like God, they left us worlds to inhabit. The worlds created by the suffering servants are described in a curious line from Psalm 34, recited daily in the Jewish tradition as part of the grace after meals: "I have been young and now I am old; yet I have not seen the righteous forsaken, nor his children begging for bread." The speaker has not seen the righteous begging for bread not because he has not looked. Nor is this line fully explained by the psalm's having a deeply mystical sense that discounts our normal meaning of the word *bread*. Rather, the psalmist is uttering the incantation of the artist: "In the world I would shape, righteousness would always be rewarded." The world of the psalmist is the world of the psalmist's vision.

The Three Transformative Ways

Now that we have an understanding of the three transformative ways, we can reinterpret all of our basic concepts in terms of one of the three ways. For example, the concept of covenant, which traditionally has been understood in terms of the obedience of the spiritual person, can with equal validity be understood as the commitment of the lover, or as the artistic medium of the artist. The greatest artists in the world are those who keep promises, because they shape their lives according to a vision of the future and overcome the impediments of a resistant medium—weak will, fatigue, and indifference—to re-create themselves as covenant keepers.

Plato has also written about the three transformative ways. "The greatest blessings come by way of madness, indeed of madness that is heaven-sent." The poet is "stimulated to rapt, passionate expression" by this madness; the prophet attests "to the superiority of heaven-sent madness over manmade sanity;" and the lover is bequeathed "a sort of madness [that] is the gift of the gods, fraught with the highest bliss."[1] Thus begins Plato's defense of love in his dialogue *Phaedrus*. The connection Plato finds among artist, prophet, and lover is an important aid in our understanding of the Hebrew Scriptures.

There are moments in which creativity takes us beyond our original conception to something previously unimagined. In the process of such creating, *we* are recreated and thus, transformed. Hence, creativity's importance as a transformative way.

The prophet sees beyond reality as it appears to us, to the deepest meaning of the present, a vision of reality as it *ought* to be. The prophetic vision results, not from the type of revelation relied upon by soothsayers, but from experiencing the deepest sources of one's being. This new understanding of one's being is the second transformative way.

The way of the lover is the route most readily open to us. What happens in love is that as we get to know the beloved in a more intimate way, we also get to know ourselves more intimately. Our loving/knowing is transformative: those we love help shape us. Hence, love is the third transformative way.

The particular transformative way we choose to emphasize in our lives depends on our own bent. We are called in ways that are consonant with our nature. Similarly, each of the major texts we have examined could be understood in terms of any one of the three ways: creativity, spirituality, or love.

For example, the text of Genesis 1 is manifestly concerned with creativity. However, we have seen that creativity is a gift of love. But Genesis 1 can also be read
as a spiritual text. It instructs us to enter into our own
tohu and *bohu*, into the formlessness and void that
underlie all thought. There, in our own emptiness, we
can touch the emptiness that preceded creation. We can
interpret the steps of creation as steps in our own
spiritual transformation, similar to those outlined by
the desert fathers.

For Jewish mystics Ezekiel 1 is a spiritual text, showing
the elements of the mystic vision. We have interpreted
the story in terms of its mandate for creativity. But it
is also understandable in terms of the way of love. The
exile, the seige of Jerusalem, and the destruction of the
Temple imply that perhaps the Children of Israel are
no longer loved by God. "The heathen are entered into
her sanctuary. . . . King and priest rejected. . . . The walls
of the city are destroyed, The gates are sunk into the
ground. . . . No vision from the Lord." But Ezekiel *has* a
vision. The very fact of renewed vision is transformative,
regardless of what that vision is. In this case, Ezekiel's
vision of the new Temple illustrates God's ongoing concern for the exiles. The terrible wound caused by this
Flood is healed by the sense of God's presence and love.

Ezekiel 40 has usually been interpreted as a spiritual
text. However, we have shown how it, too, emphasizes
the creative imagination. But the second vision of Ezekiel, no less than his first, is also a warrant for love.
So even though all the forms of our faith may have
been transformed, the text reassures us that God is ever
present and ready to accept us.

Obviously, the Song of Songs is about love. From the
first, it has also been understood as a spiritual text,
outlining the steps requisite for our spiritual transformation. This text, no less than Genesis 1, also embodies

the creative way. Our model for creativity has been based on the self-emptying and self-limitation needed to allow the creature independence. That is precisely the way that is spelled out in the text.

Exodus is a paradigm of the spiritual journey. The text also illustrates the way of love by showing that liberation occurs through love, through the acceptance of, thus the healing of, our essential wound. But Exodus is also about creation, the creation of a people and the creation of a faith.

After the Flood, God made a covenant with Noah: "Never again will I doom the earth because of man, since the devisings of man's mind are evil from his youth; nor will I ever destroy every living being, as I have done. So long as the earth endures, seedtime and harvest, cold and heat, summer and winter, day and night shall not cease." Noah was the first to plant a vineyard. He drank of the wine and became drunk because he was unable to face what we have called the Noah Paradox. But we ourselves can face it because we are now equipped with three tools for doing so: creativity, spirituality, and love.

We come to the world not to account for evil or to justify suffering; we come determined to endure with whatever has been given to us. We come ready to empty ourselves, giving totally of our being; caring, yet knowing that the world in its aliveness is free and will be what it will be. We come ready to be transformed as we seek to enter into an ever closer relationship with the whole. We come, knowing that if we are to love this world, "the miraculous quality is something one is oneself creating."[2] We come to the Noah Paradox with the realization that the solution has to do "not so much with the problem of what one seeks to find in the external world, but with what one seeks to give."[3] And we come, at last, ready to give the best of our creativity, spirituality, and love.

Notes

Introduction

1. Genesis 8:21. Quotations from the Hebrew Scriptures are generally based on the 1967 translation by the Jewish Publication Society.

1. In the Beginning

1. Samuel Terrien, *The Elusive Presence* (San Francisco: Harper & Row, 1978), 392.

2. I. Epstein, ed., *Hebrew-English Edition of the Babylonian Talmud: Ta'anith* (London: Soncino Press, 1984), Hagigah 12A.

3. *Sefer Bahir*, section 2, quoted by Alexander Altmann, "Gnostic Themes in Rabbinic Cosmology," in *Essays in Honor of J. H. Hertz*, ed. I. Epstein (London: E. Goldston Press, 1944), 27.

4. *Zohar*, Genesis, quoted in Altmann, "Gnostic Themes in Rabbinic Cosmology," 25.

2. In the Image of God

1. In Jewish mysticism the hidden God is termed *Ayen* (nothing, no thing).

2. John Chapman, *Spiritual Letters* (London: Sheed & Ward, 1935), 58.

3. Ibid., 139.

4. Lenore Friedman, *Meetings with Remarkable Women* (Boston: Shambhala, 1987), 168.

5. Talmud, Hagigah 12A.

6. Carol Ochs, *Women and Spirituality* (Totowa, N.J.: Rowan & Allanheld, 1983), 9.

7. Talmud, Hagigah 12A.

8. *Siddur,* Tefilat shaḥarit. See, e.g., *Daily Prayer Book,* ed. Philip Birnbaum (New York: Hebrew Publishing Co., 1949), 72.

9. See *Philokalia: The Complete Text,* compiled by St. *Nikodimos of the Holy Mountain and St. Makarios of Corinth,* G. E. H. Palmer, P. Sherrard, and K. Ware, trans. and ed. (London: Faber & Faber, 1979–), vol. 1, 365.

4. Another Flood

1. Jon D. Levenson, "The Jerusalem Temple in Devotional and Visionary Experience," in *Jewish Spirituality,* vol. 1, Arthur Green, ed. (New York: Crossroad, 1986), 36.

2. Bonaventure, *The Soul's Journey Into God,* in *Bonaventure* (New York: Paulist Press, 1978), 65.

3. Nachman of Bratislav, *Rabbi Nachman's Wisdom* (Brooklyn: Breslov Research Institute, 1973), 378.

4. Marion Milner, *On Not Being Able to Paint* (New York: International Universities Press, 1957), 27.

5. Bonaventure, 79.

6. Kathleen Fischer, *The Inner Rainbow* (Ramsey, N.J.: Paulist Press, 1983), 8.

7. Ibid., 9–10.

8. Abraham Joshua Heschel, *God in Search of Man: A Philosophy of Judaism* (New York: Farrar, Straus and Giroux, 1955), 46.

9. Thomas H. Green, *When the Well Runs Dry* (Notre Dame, Ind.: Ave Maria Press, 1979), 151.

10. Bernard of Clairvaux, *Selected Works,* Trans. G. R. Evans, (New York: Paulist Press, 1987), 186.

11. Susan Niditch, *Chaos to Cosmos* (Chicago: Scholars Press, 1985), 23.

12. Levenson, 37.

13. Ibid.

14. Michael Fishbane, "Biblical Prophecy as a Religious Phenomenon," in *Jewish Spirituality,* vol. 1, 74.

5. Spirituality

1. Dante, *Inferno,* trans. John D. Sinclair (New York: Oxford University Press, 1939), 23.

2. Philip Birnbaum, *The Passover Haggadah* (New York: Hebrew Publishing Company, 1953), 21.

3. Martin Buber, *Moses* (New York: Harper & Row, 1958), 58.

4. Milner, 139.

5. Jacob Needleman, *Lost Christianity* (Garden City, N.Y.: Doubleday, 1980), 177.

6. The Way of Love

1. Baruch Spinoza, *Ethics, preceded by On the Improvement of the Understanding*, ed. James Gutmann (New York: Hafner, 1955), 5.

2. *Ethics*, Book V, prop. 36, p. 213.

3. Spinoza, *On the Improvement of the Understanding*, 5.

4. Virginia Mollenkott, quoted in Emily Fowler Hartigan, "Law and Mystery: Calling the Letter to Life through the Spirit of the Law of State Constitutions," *The Journal of Law and Religion* 6 (1988): 268.

5. See note 1, above.

6. Plato *Symposium* 208b.

7. Ibid., 211.

8. Quoted in Ephraim E. Urbach, *The Sages* (Cambridge, Mass.: Harvard University Press, 1987), 454.

9. Evelyn Underhill, *The Spiritual Life* (Wilton, Conn.: Morehouse Barlow, 1955), 22.

7. Exodus in the Light of the Song of Songs

1. *Aggadot Shir ha-Shirim*, quoted in Ephraim E. Urbach, *The Sages*, 417.

2. Simone Weil, *Notebooks, 1901–1943*, trans. Arthur Wills (London: Routledge and Kegan Paul, 1956), 468.

8. In the Presence of the Flood

1. W. Gunther Plaut, ed., *The Torah: A Modern Commentary* (New York: Union of American Hebrew Congregations, 1981), 61.

2. Yaakov Culi, *The Torah Anthology: MeAm Lo'ez*, trans. Aryeh Kaplan (New York: Maznaim Publishing Corp., 1977), 1:338.

3. Nehama Leibowitz, "Midrash Rahuma," in *Studies in Bereshit Genesis*, 4th rev. ed. (Jerusalem: World Zionist Organization, 1981), 70.

4. Trevor Leggett, *Zen and the Ways* (Rutland, Vt.: Charles E. Tuttle Company, 1978), 117.

5. John S. Dunne, *The Way of All the Earth: Experiments in Truth and Religion* (New York: Macmillan, 1972; rpt. Notre Dame, Ind.: University of Notre Dame Press, 1978), 41.

6. Milner, 28.

7. Kathleen Fischer, *Winter Grace* (New York: Paulist Press, 1985), 152, paraphrasing Raymond Brown, *The Virginal Conception and Bodily Resurrection of Jesus* (New York: Paulist Press, 1973), 128–29.

8. Lynda Sexson, *Ordinarily Sacred* (New York: Crossroad, 1982), 13.

9. Oliver Sacks, *The Man Who Mistook His Wife for a Hat* (New York: Simon & Schuster, 1985), 17.

10. Ibid., 36.

9. Destruction Reconsidered

1. Gerard Manley Hopkins, *The Poems of Gerard Manley Hopkins*, W. H. Gardner and N. H. MacKenzie, eds., 4th ed. (London: Oxford University Press, 1972), 90.

2. Spinoza, *Ethics*, Part II, definition VI, p. 79.

3. Spinoza, *On the Improvement of the Understanding*, 6.

4. Milner, *An Experiment in Leisure* (Los Angeles: Jeremy P. Tarcher Inc., 1987; originally published in London: Chatto & Windus, 1937), 177.

5. Ibid., 205.

6. Ibid.

7. Cyprian Smith, *The Way of Paradox* (New York: Paulist Press, 1987), 33.

8. Milner, *An Experiment in Leisure*, 64.

9. Martin Lings, *A Sufi Saint of the Twentieth Century* (Berkeley: University of California Press, 1972), 210.

10. Milner, *An Experiment in Leisure*, 159.

11. Carol Blumenthal, unpublished manuscript, "To Harold Brown."

12. Shakespeare, *The Tempest*, Act 1, scene 2, lines 397–402.
13. Dunne, *The Way of All the Earth*, 41.

10. The One Essential Story

1. Diary entry by a fifteen-year-old girl about to be separated from her first love.
2. Poem by the same fifteen-year-old.

11. Conclusion

1. Plato, *Phaedrus*, no. 244–45.
2. Marion Milner, *On Not Being Able to Paint*, 28.
3. Ibid., 132.

About the Author

CAROL OCHS is Professor of Philosophy at Simmons College, Boston. She studied at the City College of New York and received her M.A. and Ph.D. from the City University of New York and Brandeis University, respectively. Her previous books include *Behind the Sex of God: Toward a New Consciousness Transcending Matriarchy and Patriarchy*; *Women and Spirituality* and *An Ascent to Joy: Transforming Deadness of Spirit*. She is married and has two daughters.